MW01196576

I Don't Know What To Say

Praying God's Word Over Your Home and Family

Jessica Bolyard

Author photo: Marissa Dodgen
Cover Image: Freddy Castro
Cover Design: Faith Raider
Interior Design: Jessica Bolyard

For Leah, my inspiration.

Table of Contents

If you remain in me and my words

remain in you,

ask whatever you want

and it will be done for you.

(John 15:7)

Introduction

Hello, friend. Welcome to a journey of prayer that I believe can change your home and, most importantly, the lives of those who live there.

When my daughter was a tiny baby and I was a brand new mama, praying for her every night as she slept became a priority for me. Every night, before my husband and I went to bed, I would disappear into the darkness of her room to stand over her, softly lay my hands on her back, and pray.

I prayed for her like I have never prayed for anyone else, before or since. It was a matter of urgency for me, realizing that God Himself had entrusted this tiny person to me and that I had absolutely no idea how to do what was being asked of me. I spent many cumulative hours praying and crying over her crib. I prayed like her life depended on it and, overwhelmed by the prospect of being a mother and aware of my glaring inadequacies, I truly believed that it did.

It was serious business – *even a matter of life or death* – to me, and God met me in that space as I prayed.

But then she got older. As is the case with many babies, getting her to sleep became more of a struggle. Venturing into her room *at all* once we turned off her light was risky; touching her or lingering by her bed was out of the question (unless I wanted to begin the whole bedtime routine all over again, which of course I did *not*). In that new season, my nightly prayers changed. The content was much the same, but the fervency and urgency was not. I was more comfortable with the idea of being a mama, and months of facing new experiences (good, bad, and ugly) and conquering new challenges had brought on a degree of complacency with my prayers. I may not have said it, but my attitude proudly declared, "I'm getting the hang of this, God. I can do this."

Since I already think of you as a friend, I'll be honest with you. Before long, without a sense of urgency and with a new level of comfort, my nightly prayers became a thing of the past.

In the years since then, I have repeatedly been convicted (and even ashamed) of my careless and sloppy prayer life. This is especially true as it relates to my daughter, my husband, and our home. They are the most important people in my world, and my home is our home base – our embassy where we rest from our work as ambassadors for Christ. While my conversations with my friends often (*usually*) revolve around them, I rarely talk about my family in any great depth with God. Yes, of course I pray for their health and safety and random day-to-day things they have going on, but I don't spend intentional time and effort speaking truth over their lives, boldly approaching the Throne on their behalf.

I suspect I'm not the only one. The nature of family like makes it too easy for us to take our people for granted. Things get in the way and we make the most pressing things our priorities. Grocery shopping, laundry (always with the laundry!), driving the mom taxi, carline, PTO, and somehow keeping a life of my own... It all crowds out what God calls me to do: *pray*.

If you're like me (and I suspect you may be), prayer is one of the most difficult spiritual disciplines anyway, so we start off at a disadvantage. We are commanded to pray, though, so it can't be that this is meant to be impossibly difficult. We haven't been set up for failure.

However...it can feel that way. We are in a war, friends. It's not a war with violent physical battles, but it is a very real war just the same. We have a very real enemy. We have to fight him as he comes to steal the joy and respite we experience within our homes, kill the intimacy we feel with the people we love, and destroy the beautiful structure of family as it was created to be. In this battle, prayer is our most potent weapon and, because he knows this, the enemy will do all he can to keep us from fighting on our knees.

Because this battle rages in the spiritual realm, we can be caught off guard and unequipped to handle whatever is happening around (or inside) us. Unprepared for battle, we often don't know what to say or do when spiritual situations arise in the realm of flesh and blood.

In the White House, I've learned that there is a designated room for dealing with urgent situations that arise. (Not that it's important to my point, but I learned from "Madam Secretary" that this room is called the situation room. I digress.) This is the room where, with real-time communication from around the world, the President and his cabinet can make critical decisions about things taking place in real time at home and abroad. It is very high pressure, and they can only do this because they have prepared in advance for any possible scenario. In times of lesser conflict, these men and women have dedicated themselves to learning about and preparing for *anything* that may happen. Only because they have done that can they enter the room with both a purpose and a plan. The situation is urgent and the enemy is pressing in, but preparations have already been made. Regardless of what may be going on, they are ready.

In contrast, I seem to always be facing the situations of my life completely unprepared, largely because I have spent more time worrying than praying…more time imagining what could be in my future than surrendering that uncertain future to the One who holds it in His hands. Instead of standing prepared, I am ambushed.

So the question is this: if I know this is important, which I do, why don't I pray?

I try. I do. It happens too often, though, that I sit down to pray and, because I begin with neither a plan nor a purpose, become overwhelmed by the number of things I need to cover in a limited amount of time. Words fail me and my mind wanders. I don't know what to say and eventually move on to something else, frustrated but patting myself on the back for even trying.

You, too?

Friend, the good news is that it doesn't have to be that way. God promises that when we seek Him, we will find Him. He promises that He is never far off. He promises that we face no situation alone, and that He goes before us into every situation. God promises to hear our prayers from heaven.

Because of my struggle with prayer and God's promises to me, I'm trying a more deliberate approach in my prayers for the people I love the most. I haven't come close to mastering it, but I believe it can affect how I pray, turn my heart toward God in new ways, and better prepare my family and myself for whatever lies in our futures. I believe it can do the same for you, preparing you and empowering you for every scenario. I am thrilled to be able to share what I am learning with you, namely that when I don't know what to say, the words are already there. I don't have to come up with the perfect words to bring my requests to God; rather, God's own powerful Word can speak for itself. The words are already there. I only need to know them – to be familiar enough with God's Word and His promises to call on them when I need them. That's where this book comes in.

I have selected topics and scriptures that cover many of the issues families face and that I feel called to pray over my own family. It is far from being an exhaustive list, but it is my hope that it helps to get our conversation with God going and the habit of prayer engrained in your heart and mind.

There are 31 topics organized into 31 short chapters, which I deliberately have not organized into a devotional format. After chatting with many of my friends who are wives and mamas, I've decided that I would prefer you feel equipped and empowered by God's Words than intimidated by a schedule you cannot keep. Each chapter contains an in-depth prayer referencing God's Word and His promises to us. Each verse I reference is listed in a comprehensive topical index at the back, should you be interested in looking them up for yourself.

I have also included other resources to guide you in your prayers. Pages are included throughout for your notes, specific prayers on individual topics that particularly speak to your family, ways you've seen your prayers answered, or your own journaling on the topic.

In case of inevitable emergencies and more urgent situations, I've added shorter prayers included as a quick reference in those times. You may see these prayers as more reactive than proactive; we all know that there is definitely a place in life for those prayers as well.

I've also included some of the names of God found in Scripture, along with their meanings. At times, we need reminders of who God really is so that we can approach Him confidently with our deepest needs. He knows who He is, of course, but our faith in His ability to work in our lives is strengthened when we become more aware of His character. Praying the names of God – calling to Him by what we know of Him – is a powerful way to connect with our Father.

Additionally, I've included blank pages toward the end, where you may choose to write verses of Scripture that are particularly meaningful to you as you pray, and a list of additional resources for you to consider as you take this prayer journey.

Because of this layout, the book can be used as a daily prayer guide or as a go-to reference for different situations as they come up. Either way may work for you, and that's okay. There is no right or wrong way to use this book. This is a resource, not a how-to manual.

It is my hope that this will remain a consistent habit for me, but also that it will also become a resource for you and your family as well. My thought is that this can be not only your advance preparation for life, but also your situation room-ready purposeful plan for facing it.

Regardless of how you may choose to use this resource, I am thrilled you have chosen to join me on this prayer journey. I wholeheartedly believe that it can be a transformative one for us and the ones we love.

We only need to start and keep trying. Together we can figure it out. We don't have to feel like we don't know what to say. We can become an army of wives and mamas praying God's powerful Words in unison. We can speak Truth to combat the enemy's lies. We can do this. We know what to say.

With heartfelt blessings for the journey,

Jessica

Surrendering Our Families To God

But I trust in You, Lord; I say 'You are my God'.
(Psalm 31:14)

God, You have proven Yourself trustworthy more times than I can possibly count. The entirety of Your Word tells me of Your faithfulness, and I have no reason to believe that You have anything but good things for me.

Over and over in Your Word You tell me not to fear or worry or be anxious for anything. You tell me to cast my cares on You, because You care for me. You tell me to submit to You and trust You with everything that concerns me, because what concerns me, concerns You.

I confess to You now that I have not done that with all my heart, and I have not surrendered my family to Your care.

You have promised, though, that when I cry to You, You will hear me.

You have promised that that my heart and my life are safe in Your hands.

You have promised to give me rest when I cast my burdens on You.

You have promised that when Your word lives in my heart, anything I ask of You will be done.

So Father, I surrender my family to You and place them in Your capable hands. As I begin this prayer journey, I ask for Your help in trusting You and believing Your promises. Help me to stop worrying about the future and things I cannot control, and bring me peace as I relinquish any illusion of control to which I may be clinging. It is all in Your capable hands.

Lord, I trust Your unfailing love for me and for my family. As my ancestors trusted in You, I trust You to care for the present and future generations of my family.

I give you my family, God, and ask that Your will be done.

You are the King of our home. Come, Lord.

Amen.

Praying for Salvation

For the wages of sin is death, but the gift of God is eternal life in
Christ Jesus our Lord.
(Romans 6:23)

Creator God, You created life and established Your plan for us. You allow us to choose the path we will take through life, and warn us about the consequences before we choose poorly. When we do find ourselves somewhere we shouldn't be, You have made a way for us to change direction and find the pathway to life You desire for us.

Sadly, God, none of us have chosen the best path and have wandered away from You. Your Word says that we have all fallen short and deserve the death and destruction we have chosen for ourselves. In Christ Jesus, though, You have made it possible for us to find our way back to You. In Him, You lead us to real life. Thank you for offering Your Son to save us from ourselves and our poor choices.

Today, God, I lift up my family and pray that they would choose You. I pray that they would hear Your quiet voice in their hearts, and that their hearts would be softened to the Truth. I pray that Your Spirit would convict them of their sin and of their need for a savior, and would remind them that they are never too far for You to bring them back. Help them to understand that they cannot save themselves, and that the peace they seek comes through Christ alone. Show them that as You created them in the beginning, You can recreate them now.

I pray for my husband, God, that His heart would be open to Your plan for his life. I pray that he would find new life in You. Block the plans the world has for him as he seeks You. I pray against cultural influences that tell him who he should be and what he should do, and pray that he would find his direction in Your Word.

I pray for my children, Father. Embed your Truth into their hearts so deeply that no outside influence can touch it. Help them to understand that the things they choose are often not Your best for them, and that they were made for more than the world can offer them. Help my children to grow up aware that they were created for holiness yet were born with the original sin that plagues mankind. Show them their specific sins. Show them their need for rescue, and work within their young hearts to draw them to You and the fullness of life that You offer. Father, help my family to desire You above all else.

Thank You for loving my family more than I do. Thank You for desiring more for them than I can dream. By Your power alone, draw us all into a new life with You.

You are the King of our home. Come, Lord.

Amen.

Praying for a Filling of the Holy Spirit

You, however, are controlled not by the sinful nature but by the Holy Spirit of God, if the Spirit of God lives in you.
(Romans 8:9)

Heavenly Father, today I come on behalf of my family, confessing the ways we allow worldly desires and our own sinful natures to control us. I have allowed selfish sinfulness to fill my heart and my home. I don't desire that for my family, but sometimes it is easier to passively allow things that are not of You than to press in and confront them. Please forgive me for the role I have played in allowing my family to follow their sinful natures rather than the leading of Your Holy Spirit.

Lord, as my family presses in to You and receives the new life that You offer in Jesus, I pray that my husband and my children would receive a new filling of Your Spirit. They are dead to their sins and alive only because of Christ's life in them, and the very same Spirit who raised Jesus from the dead now lives in them. They have been raised from death, but the new life they have found is fully dependent on Your Holy Spirit alive in them.

Holy Spirit, come into our home. Lead my family. Control them, not that they would be mindless and unable to make choices on their own, but that they would have the minds of Christ and the desire to choose only what He chooses. Blow through our home like a rushing wind. Rush in like an unrelenting wildfire. Burn away any hidden sin that remains, that Your Spirit would not be grieved by what is found here.

Holy Spirit, lead my husband as he leads our family. Help him to walk in confidence as he walks not in the ways of the world, but in strength that comes from Your Spirit alive in him. Give Him wisdom and guide him in everything he does. Let Your Spirit shine in and through him so that he brings light into the dark places he faces every day. As the Israelites followed pillars of clouds and fire, help my husband to have a clear sense of your leading even in the most difficult of situations. Make him bold and courageous to go against the strong current of life in this sinful world.

Spirit of God, fill my children. Let them know You well at a young age, that anything inconsistent with what You say stands out to them. Let Your Spirit of truth guide them in all they do, leading them away from anything other than Your perfect will for their lives. Help them to see Your will clearly above all else, knowing the Truth and walking freely in it. I pray against the influence of the world and their own sinful natures, and ask that You would, by Your Spirit, guide them back into Your will when they miss the mark.

Your Holy Spirit is difficult for our logical minds to understand, Lord. Silence the voice of logic and the human need to explain everything so that my family can walk in faith. Help them to believe in the inexplicable power You offer in the Holy Spirit. Help them to understand what is available to them, and teach them to rely on what they cannot see. Teach them to walk by faith and not by sight. Let them fix their eyes on things above, not earthly things, and let them be comfortable with not knowing everything.

Thank you for overwhelming us in real ways every day. Thank you for choosing us as Your temples, living inside us even in our imperfections. Change us, God, and set us apart for Your glory.

You are the King of our home. Come, Lord.

Amen.

Praying for the Fruit of the Spirit :: LOVE

Love is patient; love is kind. Love does not envy, is not boastful, is not arrogant, is not rude, is not self-seeking, is not irritable, and does not keep a record of wrongs. Love finds no joy in unrighteousness but rejoices in the truth. It bears all things, believes all things, hopes all things, endures all things. Love never ends.
(1 Corinthians 13:4-8)

Loving Father, today I place my family into Your care, and ask You to envelope them in Your perfect love. My husband and my children have been rescued by a love that has no limit, and I pray that they would come to a fresh understanding of that love and how it affects them every day.

Lord, as You live in my husband and children and Your Spirit works through each of them, I pray that my family would bear the fruit of love in their lives. I ask that my family's lives would be pure examples of love, not just in how we love the world around us, but in how we love one another. It can be easy to take each other for granted, and I pray against the spirit of complacency that lets those closest to us take the brunt of all our frustrations, stress, and troubles. You created families to be a place of intimacy and safety, so we can be our truest selves in our homes…but Jesus, even when under great pressure, didn't falter in His love for those closest to Him. Help our love for one another within these walls to be a model of Christ-like love and unity.

Help my family to be shining examples of *Your* love, not of love as the world knows it. Help them to shine with a love that stands out in its patience and kindness and selflessness and persistence and hope. Teach them to love as You have loved us, with grace, mercy, compassion, and unconditional forgiveness.

Father, help them to love with patience and kindness. Help them to bear with one another in love, enduring bad moods and hard days and harsh words without it affecting their love for one another. Create in my family a love that knows no jealousy…cannot be boastful…always puts the other person first…and shows no capacity for rudeness. Give them hearts that genuinely put their own interests behind those of others.

Help them to seek the best for other people and never demand their own way through selfishness or pride. By Your Spirit, help them to never envy, but to always rejoice with those who rejoice. Prevent them from being irritable and easily angered. Let them put unity before hurt feelings, even when it is easier to default to bitterness. Show them how to love when it is hardest, and even when it is undesirable.

Help my family to forgive and forget, keeping no remembrance of who has wronged them, and how they have been hurt. Let them learn to be as willing to move on as You are. Give them eyes that look for good, and hearts that believe the best.

Let them not tolerate gossip or slander, but help them to be vessels of truth and reconciliation. May their words be an overflow of their love for You.

Foster in them a love that never gives up, remains hopeful in every situation, and persists through even the most desperate of challenges.

Lord, as my husband and children face situations every day that, by worldly opinion, would justifiably result in hatred or fear, let their default reaction be one of love.

Gracious God, You have saved us with an unconditional and eternal love. Teach each member of my family to rest in that love. Let Your love grow within them and be carried into the world. Please let their love for people reveal Your perfect love for the world as they are models of what it means to follow You.

Thank you for loving us. On our own, we can never love the way You do, so help us all to step out of the way and allow the Holy Spirit to create the fruit of love in our lives. Help us to be changed and characterized by that love.

You are the King of our home. Come, Lord.

Amen.

Praying for the Fruit of the Spirit :: JOY

Let us run with endurance the race that lies before us, keeping our eyes on Jesus, the source and perfecter of our faith. For the joy that lay before him, he endured the cross, despising the shame, and sat down at the right hand of the throne of God.
(Hebrews 12:1-2)

Wonderful God, today I look toward the example of Your Son, and ask you humbly that my family approach life the way He did. He understood His purpose in life on Earth, but not even the tortuous anticipation of what was coming could dissuade Him from His appointed purpose. He did not allow Himself to be overwhelmed by His circumstances, but remained focused on You and Your plan for His life. He knew what was to come would be better than anything this life could give Him, and that changed everything for Him.

Really, that changed everything for *us*. Now, as we are connected again to You, allow Your Spirit to continue the work You have begun in my family, cultivating the fruit of joy in them to full completion.

There are hard, scary, and uncertain things for my husband and children to navigate every day, but they do not live as children of darkness and fear, Father. They are *Your* children. There is plenty of trouble in this world, yet in Your mercy You have assured them of Your – and *our* – victory over it all. Because of this promise and the hope they have in Christ, my family is fully able – like Christ – to be overwhelmed by Your presence in their lives, rather than being overwhelmed by their circumstances. They can rejoice in all things, trusting Your promises to them.

Father, as my husband walks through this world as a man seeking Your heart, let his joyful countenance point watching eyes back to You. I pray against discouragement, frustration, worry, anger, and stress, and ask for joy to prevail in his heart in every situation. Let Him shine as a lamp on a stand. As he lives in joy, please let him experience the peace and health that flows from a joyful heart.

A my children grow up in a world that is so radically different from any other generation, You remind me, God, that there is really nothing new under the sun. The things children today face seem more dire...more urgent...more scary than anything before in history, yet You have overcome even this. So Lord, let my children have joy, knowing in every situation that there is more happening than meets the eye. Let them have joy, understanding that a greater reward is coming as they face the challenges of standing out among their generation.

Lord, You tell us in Your Word that *You* rejoice *in us*. As hard as it is for us to imagine our own unconditional joy, the thought that we bring You that kind of joy is even more so. Let rejoicing become as natural to us as breathing. Let my husband, my children, and I be characterized by joy that raises questions and draws hearts to You.

Thank you for the hope of joy, God, and that we are not subject to the shifting sands and changing tides of the world. Our joy rests not in circumstances, but in You and Your promises to us. You are faithful, God. You are good. You are true, and have proven Your character to us time and time again. You have given us countless reasons to be joyful, so let the spark of joy be kindled in our hearts.

You are the King of our home. Come, Lord.

Amen.

Praying for the Fruit of the Spirit ::
PEACE

Therefore, since we have been declared righteous by faith, we have peace with God through our Lord Jesus Christ.
(Romans 5:1)

Father God, thank You for rebuilding the possibility of a relationship with You. In our lowest moments, You weren't preoccupied by our sin. You saw only Your precious children and longed to bring us back to Yourself. Thank You for doing that in the life and death of Jesus.

Lord, as my family grows in our faith in Christ and in their relationship with the Holy Spirit, please help them to live lives of peace. They were brought close to You as soon as they believed, and I pray that their lives would be defined by that closeness. Let there be no tension or unrest in their hearts, but only the peace that surpasses all understanding.

As my husband goes through his days as head of our family and our home, I pray that Your Spirit would fill Him with peace. The things asked and expected of him are great, and I know his heart has many opportunities to choose worry or fear over peace. I pray instead that no matter what is going on around him...no matter what particular load he is carrying...no matter what is being asked of him at any particular moment, that his heart would rest in You. That won't make everything easy, but I pray that simply knowing that he is at peace with You will put things into perspective. Grant him peace, God.

And Father, as my children face things never seen by any generation before them, please let them have peace. Let them know that they belong to the God who is in control...the God who does not abandon a work once He has begun it...the God who knit them together and sustains their every breath. Please help them to be vessels of peace in a scary world. I pray against fear, anxiety, and sadness. I pray that only the things that survive in the light would be permitted to remain.

God, because we are at peace with You, there is nothing in this world that should be able to rock our sense of wellbeing. If You are for us, nothing and no one can be against us. Please forgive us for the countless ways that we act as though we cannot trust You.

Father, thank You that we don't have to be subject to the changing winds of the world. Thank You that no matter what happens around us, we can cling to and rest in You. We are children of peace, God, and I pray that peace would overflow from us more and more every day as we go into our uncertain world.

You are the King of our home. Come, Lord.

Amen.

Praying for the Fruit of the Spirit ::
PATIENCE

Be silent before the Lord and wait expectantly for him.
(Psalm 37:7)

God, thank You for Your patience with my family and with me. We are far from the standard You have set before us for this life, yet You are unceasingly patient with our imperfections. Thank You. We certainly do not deserve Your long-suffering on our account.

I confess that I am a little nervous and have to laugh as I pray for patience for my family. I've always heard that praying for patience is dangerous, because You will give us opportunities to exercise patience when we do. But God, my family needs the patience You've promised through Your Spirit. Life is too much without it.

Father, give my family the perspective to be able to rejoice in their sufferings. I don't want them to be mindless and in denial about things happening around them, but I do want them to recognize that something bigger is at work than what they can see. Please help them to bear in mind what they know to be true about Your character as they consider the things they are experiencing. You don't change, even as they enter into the inevitable struggles of every day.

When they are in pain, Lord...when they are suffering...when they don't know how much more they can take, please give each person in my family the strength to praise You. Please help them to have real joy in the middle of their troubles, knowing that those troubles are strengthening their ability to endure. They can't know what is coming in the future, but they can know that You use all things for our good, redeem their suffering, and count every tear. Nothing they endure escapes Your notice. Let them understand that in Your economy, nothing is wasted.

Help them to keep those truths in mind when their suffering seems to go on and on, and use those truths to inspire their praise. Their situation might change, and their ability to stand under pressure might change, but You will not. You are worthy of praise.

Let it be their love for You that enables them to persevere when life is hard.

Father, help their patience in suffering to grow so that they can be strong in character, standing up to the inevitable tests that life gives them. Let their character stand out among our generation, not so that people will speak well of my family but so that people will see where their strength comes from. Let Your name be exalted in their character. Be glorified in their patience through this life.

And God, lead my husband and children through patience into hope that never wavers...never falters...never gives up. Let them have an eternal perspective, remembering always that present trials don't hold a candle to the eternal joy that awaits them in heaven. Let hope carry them through even the darkest of days.

Lord, let them suffer well. Let them keep our eyes on You, and let them be faithful no matter what they are asked to endure. Make them like Christ, who in His suffering kept His eyes on You. Let them patiently wait on You, trusting in Your promises and their past experiences of Your enduring faithfulness.

Cultivate patience in our circumstances and relationships. The Church as You designed it is made of imperfect people living alongside imperfect people, and patience is required every day. It is patience and love for one another that enables us to maintain unity within Your body.

In family relationships, we see each other in our weakest and most exhausted moments. Despite that, help our home to be a training ground for patience, that we learn relational patience here and exercise it faithfully in the world.

Thank you, Holy Spirit, for making it possible for us to suffer well and to patiently show peace and unity in a broken and divided world. By Your power at work within us, make my husband, my children, and me more patient.

Love, joy, and peace are essential to our ability to be patient, so I pray that You'd continue to cultivate those things in my family. As You have been patient with us, let us be patient in every situation and with every person we encounter.

You are the King of our home. Come, Lord.

Amen.

Praying for the Fruit of the Spirit ::
KINDNESS

And be kind and compassionate to one another, forgiving one another, just as God also forgave you in Christ.
(Ephesians 4:32)

Heavenly Father, thank You for Your abundant kindness, Your perfect compassion, and Your limitless forgiveness toward us, Your children. When we are hard to love, You remain kind. When we are suffering, You never run out of compassion. When we fail You, You open Your arms wide to forgive us. Thank You for loving us like that. Thank You for showing us that kind of undeserved kindness.

Father, I confess that for me, kindness is often hardest within my own home. I put on my best face for the world outside, but once I am home I often let down my guard and allow unkind words and attitudes to take over. Please forgive me for taking my family for granted. Please forgive me for not working harder to make our home a haven for my family. Please forgive my willingness to mutter unkind words under my breath, to be needlessly harsh when I am frustrated, to be selfish in my use of my time and energy, and to make excuses for my foul moods. I taint the image of Christ within me when I allow kindness to fall to the wayside, even within my own home. Please forgive me.

I pray today that by the power of Your Holy Spirit at work within us, my home could become a haven of kindness that feels different to my husband and children than any other place they may go. Let each member of our household feel important, cherished, and loved by the acts of kindness that define our family culture. Help each of us to seek out ways to surprise one another with kindness, that the habit would be formed at home and would carry into our interactions with the world around us. Make kindness a heart habit, rather than mental obligation.

I especially pray that my husband and children would be kind in their words and their actions. Give them eyes to see opportunities to bless others with kindness, and give them willing hearts to take action when the opportunity presents itself. Show them what it means to live out Christ-like kindness in day-to-day relationships.

Father, please help my husband to be kind in his work environment. I don't always know how men interact with one another, and I don't know the full extent of what happens during the day at his workplace. I do know, though, that in high-stress, frustrating situations, it is easy to become more task-oriented than people-oriented. It is easier to focus on the job at hand than the people standing in front of us. Please help my husband to see the people amid every problem at work. Cultivate in him a spirit of kindness toward the people he interacts with daily, always assuming the best and looking for ways to bless them.

Lord, please help my children to be vessels of kindness in an unkind world. Schools are notoriously harsh places for kids to learn how to interact with others. I pray that instead of the unkind, self-preservationist habits they can learn there, my children would introduce kindness and concern for others. Help them to shine, God. Help others to be loved by them in unusual ways, that they develop a reputation not for being "nice kids" but for being "Christlike kids".

Lord Jesus, thank You for giving us a model for living that is so vastly different than what the world offers us. We have received Your undeserved kindness in the salvation You offered us on the cross. Help us to follow in Your footsteps and to be people of other-worldly kindness.

You are the King of our home. Come, Lord.

Amen.

Praying for the Fruit of the Spirit ::
GOODNESS

For you were once darkness, but now you are light in the Lord. Live as children of light – for the fruit of the light consists in all goodness, righteousness, and truth – testing what is pleasing to the Lord. Don't participate in the fruitless works of darkness, but instead expose them.
(Ephesians 5:8-11)

Lord God, You are light. There is no darkness in You. You are good, and anything good in this world comes from You. From Your goodness, You chose to come into the darkness to get us. Thank You. Thank You for willingly entering Your creation to bring us into Your light. Let us now live as children of light, not of the darkness of the world we used to call our home.

Lord, being "good" is something we frequently ask of our children, but today I ask that You would make my family a different kind of "good". Make my family good by Your *holy* standards and make our home a holy one. There are so many ways that darkness threatens to enter our home, but I pray against that and ask for Your Spirit to usher in pure and holy light. Let there be no place for evil, for secrets, for lies, or for shame, but let those shadows dissipate as Your light shines in.

God, just like the darkness of night disappears with morning's first sliver of sunlight, I pray that Your light would expose and eliminate the fruitless deeds of darkness in our home.

Cultivate goodness in my husband, Lord. He enters into a dark world every day as he goes to work, and I pray that he would carry Your light with him as he goes. Help him to stand firmly in the light and to resist the temptations of darkness that come his way. Help him to live wisely, knowing and doing what pleases You, even (and especially) when it goes against the grain. Let him cling to good and overcome the evil around him with actions that point to You.

Father, go with my children into the world. Shine Your perfect light ahead of them, that You would clearly mark the path of goodness before them. Let them have nothing to do with the darkness they see, but help them to discern the difference between good and evil even at a young age. Help them to understand the difference between living for You and following the way of the world. Lead them to an understanding Your will and what pleases You, so that Godly goodness can become a strong feature of their character. Help them to crave Your will over what everyone else is doing...over the desire to be popular...over the desire to fit in and meet the expectations of everyone around them. Help them to trust Your way. Let them live, above all, to please You – to be children of light. Let them not just be good kids, but to be kids who manifest the goodness of their Father.

Lord, You are a good, good Father. We are Your children, so let us take after You as we run toward the light. We have all we need to do good in this world, so as we live fully equipped to reflect You, let your mercy and love shine in all that we do. Cultivate a holy goodness in my family, not that we'd be known as a good family, but that You would be known as a good God. Be glorified in us.

You are the King of our home. Come, Lord.

Amen.

Praying for the Fruit of the Spirit ::
FAITHFULNESS

Above all, fear the Lord and worship Him faithfully with all your
heart; consider the great things He has done for you.
(1 Samuel 12:24)

Father God, Your faithfulness is the foundation on which I stand, and the cornerstone of my home. I believe that You are who You have always been, and I trust that You will remain faithful to a thousand generations of my family. Thank You that when the winds of change blow through every corner of my life and nothing is certain, I can rely on Your character to remain the same. You are faithful, God. No matter what happens, that truth will light the way for me.

You, Lord, have proven Your faithfulness over and over, in Your Word and in my own life. You have been faithful to keep Your promises to Your people even when we have been unfaithful to You. Your faithfulness carried You even to a torturous death on a cross on our behalf! Lord, may the remembrance of Your faithfulness drive me to be faithful in return. May I rest in the hope that comes from knowing You are and will forever be who You say You are.

As I pray for my family today, God, I pray that the truth of Your faithfulness would be deeply ingrained in their hearts. I pray that trusting who You are would be as natural to my husband and my children as breathing. I pray that Your faithfulness would be their pathway to Your blessings.

By the power of Your Spirit, I ask You to make them faithful in every interaction and every situation, in every word and every action. Let their faith shine in everything they do, that they would be like lamps on a stand that shine brightly in a dark world and lead people to safety in You.

Lord, let my husband be found faithful as he rests in the truth and promise of *Your* faithfulness to *him*. As He is found faithful in a little, let him grow in faithfulness with more. Let him remain a man of integrity in a world that loves to see men fall, a man of honor in a world that loves to see men disgraced, and a man of respect in a world that loves to degrade men to their lowest points. I pray against the tendency of mankind to simply go with the current, and pray that he would have the strength to be faithful to You even when it is hardest. I pray that You would give my husband the will and strength of conviction to dig his feet in deeply to Your Word, that in any situations that require judgment calls or the possibility of wandering from Your will, He would stand firm. In all things and at all times, make him faithful to You, Lord.

And God, please let my children grow up knowing of Your faithfulness in their heads and experiencing Your faithfulness in their hearts. Help them to grow up learning something other than what the world teaches, so that when they are older and the stakes are even higher, they will stand firm in what they know to be true about You. Let them not be afraid of standing out, being different, or going against what their friends are doing. Let them boldly and faithfully do what they know is right because they know You are and what You have done for them. Help them to be a light in their generation, remaining faithful throughout their lives.

Help me be faithful to You and to my responsibilities to my family. Help me to rest in You and to seek only the things that You say matter. Help me to seek You and Your Kingdom first, faithfully pursuing You in all that I do.

Let our home be a training ground for faithfulness, God. Show me my part in making that happen. Let us be faithful to You in all we do, as You have never wavered in Your faithfulness to us.

You are the King of our home. Come, Lord.

Amen.

Praying for the Fruit of the Spirit ::
GENTLENESS

Therefore I, the prisoner in the Lord, urge you to live worthy of the calling you have received, with all humility and gentleness, with patience, bearing with one another in love, making every effort to keep the unity of the Spirit through the bond of peace.
(Ephesians 4:1-3)

Heavenly Father, I thank You today for Your gentleness in coming in the person of Jesus. You willingly stepped from Your throne into our broken world, never considering Yourself too good to come into Your creation as a helpless baby. Thank You for being gentle with us when our hearts are hostile and our spirits are rebellious. You came not in anger, frustration, or wrath, but in tenderness and love. You came not to assert Yourself in power, but to reveal Your affection for your people. You came not with thunderous fanfare, but in the quiet of a winter breeze. Thank You for being gentle with our hearts when we deserve harsh discipline.

I pray today, God, that through Your Spirit, my family would bear the same fruit of gentleness we see in Jesus. I ask not that You would make them spineless and weak, but that in Christ-like meekness they would consider others over themselves. Help them to have Jesus's gentleness of spirit, speaking with kindness and love in all situations.

Lord, as my husband goes through his days, help him to be gentle. The world's way for men is to create a name for themselves through power and position. Instead, I pray that his life would be about making a name for *You* through humility and gentleness. Help him to be bold in going against society's expectations and seeking out Your purpose for his life, but gentle in his way of living it out. I pray that in difficult conversations, he would put others first, hearing them out and responding as Jesus would. I pray that in difficult situations, he would seek Your guidance before the insight of others. I pray that in matters of character, he would seek to model himself after You before the examples he sees around him. Generate in him a desire for Your Spirit, not to be known for his own power but by his gentleness in character. Let his gentleness be seen by the people he encounters, and let Your name be glorified.

And Father God, please help my children to learn gentleness. Let their actions and words be seasoned with love and mercy. As they are faced with bullies and difficult people, help them respond like Jesus. If they are in situations they've never faced before, help them to look to Jesus above their instincts or the advice of others. Let their daily interactions be characterized by their gentle and quiet natures, making them known for having gentle spirits like You --- not just as "nice kids".

Lord, You have come to unite us under the Spirit. I pray that through the power of that Spirit, You would cultivate the fruit of gentleness in my family. Let us be agents of unity and love in a world that seeks to divide and conquer. Help us to act in gentle humility, loving the world as You do and bringing honor to Your name.

You are the King of our home. Come, Lord.

Amen.

Praying for the Fruit of the Spirit ::
SELF-CONTROL

A man without self-control is like a city broken into and left without walls.
(Proverbs 25:28 ESV)

Gracious, merciful Father, thank You for Your gifts to us. I am quick to thank You for Your gifts of grace and salvation and for things I *observe* during my days, but I often forget to thank You for some of the things that actually *carry me* through those days. You are faithful to give me all I need for every situation I face, and are always available for me to lean on and find strength in. Thank You for sending Your Spirit to us, and thank You for the incredible possibilities in our lives because of His presence in us.

Lord, You promise that as the Spirit works in our willing hearts, self-control will become evident in our lives. I confess, though, that sometimes that is hard to imagine. It is far too easy to give in to the impulsive desires that come so naturally and the thoughts that seem to run rampant in my mind. Self-control seems like an impossible goal.

With You, though, nothing is impossible – even self-control. So God, as Your Spirit moves within our home, teach my family to be self-disciplined. Train them in *Your* discipline, so they are led not by their selfish desires, fear, or need for control but by Your Spirit. I ask that they would be disciplined and engaged in following You with every part of their being. Let them learn to control their minds first, before anything else. Their words and actions flow from the thoughts they allow, so please make those thoughts like Yours.

You promise that we have everything we need to become self-controlled followers of You. You promise that Your strength is made perfect in our weaknesses, and that we can do all things through You. You promise that as we turn our hearts toward You, You will change us by the power of Your Spirit, not by any effort of our own. You promise that in a self-controlled life are many blessings.

Because we believe Your promises, I pray, Father, that You would train my family in your self-control. I long for them to be conformed to the pattern You set before us.

God, please work in my husband and children to cultivate self-control. It truly is a gift to be able to live from something higher than instinct or knee-jerk reactions. Thank You that we aren't enslaved by our sin, but that we are adopted by You – and that You have overcome this world. Help my family to walk in truth, seeking You and carrying Your light into the world as they live self-controlled lives, ultimately surrendered to You.

You are the King of our home. Come, Lord.

Amen.

Praying for an Attitude of Prayerfulness

Pray constantly.
(1 Thessalonians 5:17)

Eternally merciful God, thank You for the direction You give to help us navigate life in this world. You give us hope that what we see isn't all there is, patience to endure life's inevitable hardships, and a way to connect with You through it all in prayer. Thank You for desiring that time with us, both in conversation and silence. Thank You for prayer, and for the utter miracles it can do in our lives.

Father, please let prayerfulness become a natural habit for my family. Take them all beyond shallow, ritualistic prayer into a life of constant communion with You. Please forgive me for my halfhearted approach to prayer and teach me a new way. I confess that this is something I struggle with (hence this journey through prayer), and I have not always set a good example for my family. Show *me*, first, what it means to pray without ceasing and to trust in You, that I may experience You more fully and may be an example to those I love.

I pray that my family would become a family of prayerfulness. If we develop a reputation for that, let it only declare the faithful trustworthiness of the One to whom we pray. Help us to grow in our lives of prayer, recognizing the obvious needs we see and the subtle prompts of the Spirit to seek You in prayer moment by moment.

Let my family's prayers teach them more of who You are, and let them meditate on the Truth of Your Word. Let prayer be a reminder to ourselves that there are so many things we are incapable of doing, but that You make all things possible in Christ. Let that promise lead us to boldness in our prayers. As they pray in complete confidence, Lord, please make my husband and children like trees planted alongside a spring, standing strong with deep roots and bearing fruit in every season.

As for my husband, help him to work through any issues and struggles he may have with prayer and enter a new relationship with You through his prayers. Father, take him beyond the most basic prayers of request into prayers of genuine communion. Remind him to be quiet in prayer, letting his spirit commune with Yours in an intimate way, conforming his will to Yours as his heart is changed. Teach him the discipline of both intentional stillness and of continual prayer while he goes about his days.

Father, please help my children to learn the value of prayer from a young age. The abstractness of it can even be hard for adult minds to grasp, so I ask You to make prayer a natural way of life for them while they are young. Help them to feel Your closeness as they pray and sense the power of their words.

God, change my family through prayer in a way that is undeniable. Help us to understand the way You desire for us to live in prayerfulness, and then change the trajectory of our lives through our ongoing conversations with You. Aware of the weakness of our flesh, let us lean on You in prayer; let us be made strong to stand against the temptations of this world.

Teach us to pray as Jesus did, saying, "Father, may Your name be honored as holy. Your kingdom come. Give us each day our daily bread. And forgive us our sins, for we ourselves also forgive everyone in debt to us. And do not bring us into temptation, but deliver us from the evil One." Yours is the Kingdom, the power, and the glory forever and ever.

You are the King of our home. Come, Lord.

Amen.

Praying for Trust in God

Trust in the Lord with all your heart, and do not rely on your own understanding; in all your ways know Him, and He will make your path straight.
(Proverbs 3:5-6)

Gracious God, thank You that we can trust You with the daily workings of our lives. A lesser love might step back at a distance and force us to figure things out on our own, but Your perfect love offers guidance and direction for every situation.

Father, I pray today that my family would grow in their trust of You. I pray that in every situation life brings, they would rest securely in Your promise that You love them, want only the best for them, and will use every situation in their lives for their ultimate good.

Our understanding of the world is so narrow, so I do pray that You would help my family to see from Your perspective and grow in wisdom. As they grow in Your wisdom, though, let them never believe they can rely on their own understanding or their own strength, but to humbly keep their eyes on You.

I pray against *any* tendency to take things into their own hands, believing they can rely on their own strength. Throughout Scripture there are countless examples of people who didn't trust You – didn't believe Your promises – didn't want to wait for Your methods or Your timing. It has happened over and over in my own life, too! It never works out well, God, so I pray that my family would learn from those examples. I pray, too, that Your Spirit would make them aware of the times in their lives when they have tried or are trying to force Your hand and make things happen the way they want. Please forgive them for those times, because the root of it all is pride and their disbelief that You are who You say You are.

I pray one of the most vulnerable prayers I can pray my family: keep them humble, God. Give them a proper understanding of who You are and their relationship to You, their all-powerful Creator God. As they grasp your majesty little by little, let them feel no distance from You but confidence that they can lean into You.

I pray, Lord, that my husband and children would acknowledge You in everything they do – that no area of their lives would be off-limits to You. Let them wholly commit everything they have to You, holding no piece of their hearts back from You as they trust You and Your plans for their lives.

Keep my husband from walking through this life as the world tells him to. Men are "supposed" to act quickly and with authority, but I pray that my husband would instead trust You and wait for Your timing. Help him to act decisively when the situation requires it, but always based on Godly wisdom, discernment, and trust in You instead of his own knowledge or understanding.

Please let my children grow up with an increasingly intimate awareness of You at work in their lives. Help them to see that Your ways are not always what they would choose, but they are always perfect. Help them look to You for guidance and wisdom in every situation, trusting You to say, "This is the way. Walk in it." Show me my role in teaching them how to acknowledge You.

As I pray over my home today, I pray against fear, because it goes against everything You have promised. It is a thief and one of the go-to weapons of our enemy, and it is so often our default reaction in times of uncertainty. Fear gives the illusion that we have some degree of control over our situations, steals the joy from our days, and makes us forget the gifts You have given us.

So I pray that in my home, there would be no place for fear – only for trust in the good and perfect gifts You have given. Protect my family from the anxieties and fears of life in this increasingly dark world, and help them to walk in truth. Help them to walk in trust when it doesn't make sense, instead of pursuing the easier routes of panic and worry.

Gracious Father, we have no way of knowing what lies ahead of us on this journey, but You see the whole path with perfect clarity. Help my family to walk that path with trust and full acknowledgement of who You are. Direct our paths, Father, and let us trust Your promises more than our own understanding. You are God and we are not.

You are the King of our home. Come, Lord.

Amen.

Praying for Strength in Difficult Times

God is our refuge and strength, a helper who is always found in times of trouble.
(Psalm 46:1)

Father, You are so good. In every situation we face, no matter how uncertain or scary or unpredictable, we know that you are always the same...always certain...always good. Thank You for being our anchor in the waves...our lighthouse in the storm...our fortress in every attack of the enemy. You are the rock we can lean on when everything else gives way.

Searching Your Word for the word "strength" leads mainly to verses telling of Your faithfulness and Your promises, rather than instruction on how to be strong. There is a reason we are reminded more of who You are than of what we should do: nothing we do could compare in power to who You simply *are*.

So God, I pray today that my family would find their strength in You no matter what situations they may face today, tomorrow, or further down the road.

It's too easy to rely on our own efforts and abilities, but Lord, our limitations set in so quickly that we realize again how we just don't have what it takes. In You, though, they can do all things. Help them to reach the end of themselves so that they begin to learn more of who You are. May that knowledge lead them to praise with their whole heart, mind, and soul.

You promise us that in our weaknesses, Your power is made perfect, and that when we feel weakest You will make us strong. I certainly don't pray for hard things to enter the lives of the people I love, but I do pray that in whatever they encounter, they wouldn't fight their weaknesses. I pray that they would accept and even lean into their weaknesses and limitations, allowing You to work and the world to see You more clearly. And God, when they reach the other side of their battles, may they stand in victory and give praise to You alone.

Lord, I pray that You would strengthen my husband for the daily struggles of being a man in this world. I will never fully comprehend the burden he bears, but I find comfort knowing that You *do* understand. You have walked through life as a man, and You know all that he faces, so God, please give him the strength he needs. Help him to lean on You instead of himself. Let him humbly ask You for help. Help him to be a model of biblical manhood, embracing his weaknesses and letting them show...all so that You can be glorified.

Father God, I ask You to please give my children strength to thrive in every situation they encounter. Let them realize at an early age that their weaknesses are not flaws, as the world may see them, but are amazing opportunities for You to show Yourself to them.

Show them the particular struggles that You want to use for Your glory, and help them to rely on Your strength in those areas.

Please let my family stand strong, God. There are strong winds of culture that threaten to uproot them, but I pray that they would be so deeply planted in You that nothing can sway them. Help them to always seek Your face, knowing that You are an ever-present help in times of trouble. Hold on to my family, God. Let their strength come from You, and may You be forever glorified in their lives.

You are the King of our home. Come, Lord.

Amen.

Praying for Wisdom in Decision-Making

Whenever you turn to the right or to the left, your ears will hear this command behind you: "This is the way. Walk in it."
(Isaiah 30:21)

Gracious Father, thank You for sending Your Son to rescue us from the ways of the world. We didn't even realize that we needed to be saved, but in grace and mercy You came and drew us into life and truth as only You can. Thank You for not giving up on us, and thank You for patiently offering a better way to live. You are the Creator of life itself, and I praise You for designing us with such a perfect plan in mind.

Lord, I pray today that You would strengthen my family for decisions they make. The current of culture is strong, Lord, but I pray that they would remain firmly grounded in You and unmoved by the ways of the world. Let them delight in You more than they delight in the world so that their roots would dig deeply into Truth and make them unwaveringly strong. I know they face situations and decisions even today that require them to choose the way of culture or the way of Christ, and I ask You today to give them strength to make the wise choice, trusting Christ in everything.

I know that we don't have to earn Your love or be worthy enough, somehow, for Your grace to find us, but I pray that as my family moves forward in difficult situations, their actions, words, and mannerisms would be worthy of the name of Jesus. Above all else, let them show You to the world and turn the eyes of a watching world to You – the giver of all good things.

Father God, please help my husband, in his job and his leadership of our family, to make decisions that align with the gospel of Christ. Help him to be unmoved by influences around him. Help him to stand strong when choosing Your way makes him unpopular. Help him to walk through each day with the integrity and strength of character modeled by Jesus. Create a spirit of radical obedience within him, Lord, that he would be so focused on what You ask him to do that nothing else is an option. Give him strength of conviction, Lord.

I ask You to please build up my children in their belief and convictions, so that when those beliefs are challenged they respond with confidence and love. Let my children be known for strength of conviction, and let them remember always that you fight for them and are on their side in every struggle. I pray that by their own experiences of You they would be more trusting of *Your* way than in whatever options the world offers them. Let them remain strong against the current of culture, and guide them in wisdom for every counter-cultural decision they make.

Thank You, Father, for sending Your Spirit to live within us as we face each day. In everything, let us choose the way of truth, wisdom, humility, honesty, and light. Please help us to tune our hearts to You, that we would miss no promptings of Your Spirit and no opportunities to shine the light of Christ around us.

You are the King of our home. Come, Lord.

Amen.

Praying to Live for God, not Man

Am I striving to please people? If I were still trying to please people,
I would not be a servant of Christ.
(Galatians 1:10)

Gracious Father, thank You for reaching out and taking hold of us. Thank You for going to unfathomable lengths to draw us back to You, and thank You for not giving up on us while we waited to make a decision. Thank You for not giving up on us every day, while we stumble and falter and do such a poor job of living for You and our created purpose.

Lord God, I pray that my family would live for *Your* approval only. The approval of others is always up ahead, like a carrot dangling, and they will never quite reach it. The expectations of the world are always changing and are relentlessly demanding, but Your yoke is easy and Your burden is light. Help them to find true life and real satisfaction in You alone.

Let them stand on the stage of life and see no one in the audience but You, and as they walk through the different scenes of life let them sense Your Spirit always cheering and encouraging them on.

I pray, God, that none of the accolades of the world would mean anything if they don't feel that they are in line with Your will. Let them have life, and life to the full as they live for you. And let them live for You first, God. *You first*. What good is it if they gain the whole world but lose their souls?

And Father, even as they seek Your approval, let them have a soul-deep understanding that You love them unconditionally and irrevocably. Let them understand that they cannot earn salvation or any more of Your love, but that they can walk in humble obedience and earn the prize You have for them in heaven. Let them always remember that though they may make mistakes, they are always pre-approved in Your eyes. Remind them that nothing can change Your love for them or Your appointed purpose for them.

Walk with my husband and children through their most challenging days, Lord, and help them to walk in confidence knowing that they have the Creator of the universe at their backs. Let them chase after Your will, God, instead of compliments or acceptance from the people around them. Help them to be bold in following You, especially when it means they will be misunderstood or rejected.

Encourage their spirits when they are mocked or excluded. Lift them up when they are hated for their refusal to live by the world's rules. As the world hated Jesus, they may be hated for loving Him. Encourage them, God, and remind them that they have a great high Priest who understands every struggle.

Lord, I pray sincerely that my family would not fall into the traps of society and culture.

Let them live for You, and let Your approval be more than enough. Let my family be salt and light in among people who seek to impress and outdo and fit in.

You are the King of our home. Come, Lord.

Amen.

Praying for Resistance to Temptation

No temptation has come upon you except what is common to humanity. But God is faithful; he will not allow you to be tempted beyond what you are able, but with the temptation he will also provide a way out so that you may be able to bear it.
(1 Corinthians 10:13)

God, You are good. You are faithful. You are merciful and compassionate and gracious. In every situation, You are the light that shines to pierce the darkness and the truth that silences all other voices. You are my strength to stand and my rest when I lie down.

Father, thank You for Your wisdom. You knew before you created us that we would fall away, so in Your perfect love You already had a plan to draw us back before we ever strayed. You provide a way out for every temptation we face, never wanting to abandon us in a time of need and always keeping the road open for us to come running back to You. And Lord, thank You for never giving us more than we can handle...*without Your help.*

Thank You, Lord, for freeing us from our sinful natures. Thank You for breaking the chains that enticed us and dragged us away from You.

I pray for my family today, God, that they would draw close to You so that they can clearly hear and recognize Your voice. The more clearly they can hear Your voice, the more ridiculous all the voices of the world will sound. Help my husband and children to pull into You daily, before the noise and clamor of the world begin. Help them to be so acclimated to the sound of Your voice that they immediately recognize when You speak and never hesitate to respond in obedience.

Let my family not be enticed by the desires of their sinful natures. Lead them into Truth, not temptation. Conform their hearts and minds to Yours, that the greatest desires of their hearts are in line with Yours. Help them to resist the instant gratification the world offers for their every appetite and craving. Teach them patience and strength in the face of temptations that seem too much for them. Show them Your sufficiency, and please help them to humbly ask Your help when they are struggling to choose the right way.

Gracious Father, the way men are made puts my husband at risk for temptations that as a woman, I will never be able to understand. I know, though, that the enemy seeks to use the perfect way You designed men to attack them at every opportunity. Guard my husband's eyes, Lord, and protect his mind from the attacks of the enemy. Give him the discernment to take every thought captive to Christ before it can take up residence in his mind. Help him to resist temptations of the flesh, relying on Your Spirit to pull him through every moment of weakness. Help him to learn from and be encouraged by the temptation of Christ, knowing that he faces nothing that Christ Himself did not face or cannot understand.

Father, please help my children to resist the temptations of youth. Peer pressure is a very real threat to a child's identity. Help my children to be grounded in who *You* say they are, so that they are less likely to find their identity in who culture says they are or should be. Help them to see themselves as Your children. Give them wisdom and strength to withstand the inevitable situations they will face, and help them to stand strong in Your truth. Your Word and Your love can light the way for them; help them to choose to follow You when they don't know the way.

Gracious God, You do not tempt, but You provide us a way out when the tempter comes. He comes when we are weakest, attacking us in our weakest places. Help my family to follow the model of Christ when our enemy presses in, wielding our swords of truth as expert warriors. You've given us a full set of armor to fight the spiritual battle before us. Protect my family, God, and give them the strength to fight for what is right. Let them stand strong against the temptations and plans of the enemy.

You are the King of our home. Come, Lord.

Amen.

Praying for the Protection of Family Relationships

If a house is divided against itself, that house cannot stand.
(Mark 3:25)

Heavenly Father, thank You for my family. Because the very first relationships You established at creation were that of marriage and parenthood, we know You intended them to be good and perfect gifts to us. Even more, since You choose to be known as our Father and have adopted us as Your children, Your love for us and the love that should exist within families is clear. Each relationship within my family is precious; let me never take them for granted.

And God, since You intend families to be a gift, I know, too, that my enemy wants to distort that gift in any way he can. He seeks to kill and destroy any beautiful thing You have established. I realize he will use any means necessary to do that, and division is one of his favorite weapons.

But Lord, I pray today for unity within my family. Please protect my family from those attacks. It is tempting every hour of every day to take the easy road...to live for ourselves...to put our own wants before those of the people we love. I ask that we would not give in to the temptation to seek our own best interest first. Conflicts are inevitable, but I pray that no conflict or disagreement would be strong enough to break the bonds You have established.

Keep the words and thoughts pure within our home, God. Lead my family away from the temptation to speak badly of one another. Regardless of our surroundings or who we are with, let the only words my husband, my children, and I speak about each other be edifying. By Your Spirit, let each member of our family build one another up in our speech and actions. Help our minds to be focused on whatever is true, honorable, just, pure, lovely, commendable, excellent, or worthy of praise, and help our words reflect those things.

I pray against the plot of the enemy to drive a wedge between my husband and me. Our marriage is a cord of three strands, and with You in the center nothing can break us apart. You have bonded us together as one flesh – merged our lives and futures together as one – and none of the powers of darkness can separate what You have united. Help us to remain a unified front in all things. I pray, God, that in even our most difficult conversations Your Spirit of love and truth would prevail. Help us to unite our hearts with Yours, and thereby to be united with one another. I pray that just as Christ cannot be separated from His Church, we cannot be separated from one another, and that as we grow closer to You we would grow closer to one another. Lord, let us always be on guard against those things that could come between us.

As our children grow up, grow a relationship of mutual respect and love between us. I pray that we would develop relationships of trust that cannot be broken, that communication would remain open, and that we would all always assume the best about one another. Do not allow distrust, suspicion , or self-centeredness to have a place in our home.

God, while the world has its own ideas of what family should look like, let my family be an encouraging model of the way family relationships can be. Let what people see on the outside be consistent with what is happening in our home. Please help us to be salt in the world, adding flavor and preserving what You intended life to be.

Lord, the members of my family each come against opposition in so many forms out in the world. Let our home, though, be a sanctuary of safety and love. Let nothing internal or external, real or imagined, physical or spiritual come between the people You have placed in my life and me. Nurture those relationships, God. Thank You for my family. Watch over our relationships, and let us guard them as fiercely as a lion.

You are the King of our home. Come, Lord.

Amen.

Praying for an Attitude of Servanthood

Do nothing out of selfish ambition or conceit, but in humility consider others as more important than yourselves. Everyone should look out not only for his own interests, but also for the interests of others. Adopt the same attitude as that of Christ Jesus. (Philippians 2:3-5)

Heavenly Father, I thank You for Your willingness to lower Yourself to be with us. You could have stayed away and not become involved in our mess. You could have remained at a distance appropriate for Your majesty and holiness. You could have left us to figure things out on our own. Instead, though, You put Your majesty aside to walk among us in the person of Jesus. I thank You for not abandoning us in our sin. Thank You for not seeing our brokenness as reason to distance Yourself from us, but as an opportunity to serve us. Thank You for Your perfect love.

Please help my husband and children to have the minds and hearts and attitudes of Christ. Please keep my husband and children from looking to their own interests, but to the interests of others. Lord, help them to see other people as more important than their own needs, comfort, plans, or desires. In every situation, let them be the ones looking out for the interests of the underdog...fighting for the rights of the victims...speaking up for the voiceless. Let them go to uncomfortable places and do uncomfortable things because their own comfort isn't as important as serving others. Let them live for an audience of One – wanting approval only from You.

Let my family always be willing to become involved in those things in which Jesus would be involved. Help us to walk through life with the eyes and ears and attitudes of Jesus, seeing and hearing and seizing opportunities to love and serve. If it is somewhere You would be, let us be there, too. If it is a situation You would become involved with, let us put ourselves out there. If there is a person who You would gravitate toward, let us be with them, too.

Let my husband, my children, and me never think of ourselves as higher, better, or more important than anyone or anything. Rather than adopting the worldly attitude of selfish ambition and vanity, let us instead see others as better than we are. May the special gifts and talents You have given each of us be put to use in service to You and the world.

Father, while I desire for my family to serve the world, I pray, too, that an attitude of humble service would permeate our home, too. Let my family members seek, even in times of rest, to give themselves up for someone else. Because my children look to me as an example, let me be selfless as I serve You by serving the people around me.

God, thank You for the example You set for us in Jesus. Thank You for not just asking us to do something, but also demonstrating how to do it. Remembering all that You have done for us leads us to do wonderful things for You. Thank You for Your Word, lighting the way and showing us just how to go about Christ-like living. You are a good, good Father, and it is our joy to serve You with all our hearts, souls, and strength.

You are the King of our home. Come, Lord.

Amen.

Praying for Wisdom

*For wisdom is better than jewels, and nothing
desirable can equal it.
(Proverbs 8:11)*

Eternal Father, I am so thankful for Your wisdom. When we think we know what we need, You give us what is best. When we think we know where to go, You lead us in the better way. When we think we know the right way, You point us in the other direction....or wait until we decide to listen. Thank You for You infinite wisdom, patience, and mercy.

God, I pray today that You would give wisdom to my family. Please help them to see with eyes of understanding and clarity. Help them to see as You do, rather than as the world does. Help them to deeply understand that Your ways are higher than theirs, and Your thoughts are higher than even the wisest thought they can conceive. Cut down all evidence of pride in their lives, that they would be willing to hear Your wisdom and accept correction.

Be with my husband in every decision...every situation...every interaction he faces. Help him to have the kind of unshakeable clarity of mind that comes from You. Please let him walk into dark or confusing situations with insight from You, knowing without a doubt that Your wisdom will not fail. Help him to be a man of wisdom, planted by a stream with deep roots and bearing fruit in every season. Let His relationship with You lead to greater wisdom, and greater wisdom to lead to a deeper relationship with You. Create in Him a holy cycle of reverence and wisdom.

Lord, please let my children grow in wisdom even as they grow in physical size. Help them to adopt Your wisdom rather than that of the world. There are a million things around them every day that want to direct their paths, but only wisdom from You will lead them down the path to life. Help them to know the difference. Help them to hear and recognize wisdom from You in the middle of a noisy world that thinks it knows what is best for them. Let them listen to Your Word instead, and let them heed our instructions as their parents...but only as far as the wisdom in those instructions comes from our own relationships with You.

Merciful God, thank You for faithfully giving wisdom to those who ask for it, hiding and revealing the depths of Your wisdom in Christ. I ask You now to please help my husband and children to learn to walk in wisdom. Make them wise in Your eyes first, not their own or those of the world. Let their purity, peacefulness, respect, submissive spirits, mercy, fruitfulness, impartiality, and sincerity grow as they grow in wisdom. Please give them the fullest measure of Your infinite wisdom that their finite minds can bear.

You are the King of our home. Come, Lord.

Amen.

Praying for a Spirit of Humility

Humble yourselves before the Lord, and He will exalt you.
(James 4:10)

Father God, You created us, redeem us, and sustain us. You guide us through this life as our Shepherd, protecting us from harm and disciplining us when we wander. You are our comfort, and Your mercy leads us to places of rest in times of suffering. You provide...You lead...You comfort, all out of Your goodness, faithfulness, and relentless love for us.

Lord, when we stop to recognize who You are, we fall to our knees and see again what we are: dust...a vapor...a flicker in the realm of time. It is amazing that You would preoccupy Yourself with us. And yet, Lord, when we get into day-to-day life, it becomes too easy to think more of ourselves than we ought. We think we can handle everything. We think we are strong enough and know enough and can manage on our own. Please forgive us for our prideful, self-reliant tendencies.

I ask today that You would help my family to humble themselves before You, God. Make them aware of their sin and their need for You. Let there be no place in our home for selfish pride or ambition, but only for sincere humility of spirit. Help my husband

and my children to lower themselves voluntarily, that their pride doesn't necessitate a fall. Let them look at the world from a lowly vantage point, never assuming that they are higher or more important than they really are. Let them have the attitude and humility of Christ at all times.

Lord God, You promise to lift us up when we lower ourselves, but that is not why I seek humility. I seek humility for my family so that they can see You more clearly...know You more dearly...feel You more nearly. I pray that my husband and children would be constantly stepping out of the way to let all eyes be on You.

Father, I ask that You would please grow an attitude of humility in our home and our hearts. Let us be as humble and gentle with one another as we would be with those outside our home. We are Your children, and when we begin to think of ourselves as more, please humble us. Let us take on the attitude of Christ, walking humbly with You, so that we can accurately and fully represent You to the world.

You are the King of our home. Come, Lord.

Amen.

Praying for Awareness of Spiritual Gifts

Now concerning spiritual gifts: brothers and sisters, I do not want you to be unaware.
(1 Corinthians 12:1)

Heavenly Father, thank You for giving us Your Spirit to equip us as we walk through this life.

Thank You for coming to dwell inside of us, helping us to walk in supernatural power and experience You intimately.

Thank You for giving us gifts straight out of Your nature to advance our experience and understanding of You, allowing us to spread that understanding to others.

Thank You for giving us a part in building and expanding the Body of Christ throughout the world. It is a privilege and an honor to serve You, and it is humbling to realize that You have designed each of us to do a specific job within this Body.

Holy Spirit, I thank You for giving us Your gifts for distinct purposes and holy callings. It is by Your grace that we don't live aimlessly and without a sense of mission. Thank You for knitting us together the way that You did, Lord, and for creating us anew in Christ Jesus to do the good words You planned long ago for us to do. We truly are Your masterpieces, God. Help us to see ourselves that way.

Father, I pray today that my family – each member, from the youngest to the oldest – would come alive in a new awareness of their place in Your Body. I pray that my husband and my children would dig deeply into who *You* are to discover who You have made *them* to be.

Help them to realize what beautiful gifts You have given them, God, and help them to embrace them without fear as they rest in Your perfect love. I pray that my family would lean in to their callings, despite their fears. Empower them to act on their gifts. I pray that they would trust Your design and press in to You, for You created them on purpose, for a purpose. Let them embrace and trust their gifts, Lord, and You for giving them.

And Father, I pray that they would learn to walk by the power of Your Spirit. Help my husband and children not walk by their own strength or abilities, but to walk in faith believing that their gifts aren't reliant on their skills. Help them to fearlessly exercise their gifts, experiencing the fullness of Your Spirit as Your power is made perfect in their weaknesses. Help them to simply be obedient in the use of their gifts, and help them to relinquish the results into Your capable hands.

Holy Spirit, show them how important their gifts are to the entire Body. Let them never see their particular gifts as inferior or less important, but help them to understand that without them, the Body of Christ would suffer. May they use their gifts both to minister to the Body, equipping it for ministry, and to make You known by their faithfulness to the Gospel of Christ.

I pray that as my husband and children discover more about how they are made, they would eagerly pursue opportunities to exercise their gifts for the benefit of the Body. I pray that as my children begin to understand how their talents, abilities, and passions connect to the specific calling You have on their lives, that You would help them to walk in bold confidence knowing that though they are young, they are important to the story of the world.

Father, let us not walk by sight. We may not look like the world's idea of prophets, preachers, teachers, or shepherds, but we believe that Your Spirit breathes those gifts into us. Help us to walk in faith that we are chosen for Your purposes. I ask all of this, God, not so that we would appear successful by the world's standards or receive accolades for ourselves, but so that we would learn humble reliance on Your Spirit as He works within us. Help my family to experience You deeply and intimately as we do things we simply cannot do on our own power. Thank You for this incredible opportunity to play a part in Your story. Be glorified as we learn our roles in it.

You are the King of our home. Come, Lord.

Amen.

Praying for a Sense of Purpose and Calling

*For we are God's masterpiece. He created us anew in Christ Jesus,
so we can do the good things he planned for us long ago.
(Ephesians 2:10 NLT)*

Lord God, You created each of us on purpose with a specific plan for our lives. You have knit us together intentionally and deliberately, and I praise You for the knowledge and wisdom that went into making us who we are.

Father, I pray today that my family would believe that they are Your masterpieces and rest in that truth. There are plenty of conflicting messages in the world, telling them who and what to believe about themselves, and I pray that they would have a deep and abiding belief that they are who You say they are. Please help them to see themselves through Your eyes – not as failures or disappointments, but as Your children deliberately designed for a beautiful purpose.

Lord God, please help my husband and children to develop a real sense of what their purpose might be in this world. Help them to know that they were made, first, for an intimate relationship with You, and let that be what motivates everything else. Please help them to understand that they are not an anonymous face in the crowd, but that they are Your precious, beloved children. Help them to know how special they are to You – special enough to be considered Your masterpiece among all of the incredible things You have made. Special enough to be chosen. Special enough to be given the privilege of seeing You. Special enough to represent You to the world.

Father, please help my husband and children to be driven by a real sense of calling. Help them to understand that beyond Your calling on them as Your children, You have a job for them – and only them – to do in this world in order to fulfill Your purposes. Let them not be as concerned with their own dreams as they are with Your plans. In the deep places of their hearts, conform their plans to Yours. Show them what it means to be fruitful for You.

Help my family to come to a clear understanding of their gifts, talents, and passions, and how You intend to use them in their lives. Help that awareness to motivate them to be the very best version of themselves that they can be – not for their own reputations or image, but to be a light as they follow in the footsteps of Jesus.

I ask You to affirm the callings and purpose of my husband and children. Help them to know that whatever they feel called to do in life, it is monumentally important when they commit their work to You and do it for Your glory. Help them to find meaning in the mundane aspects of life, too, Lord, that their time here in this life is not wasted.

Help my husband, children, and me to understand that it is not by our power that Your purposes will prevail. While You do not need to use us, You choose to. What a privilege!

As we pursue You, let my family respond to Your voice as Samuel did: "Speak...Your servant is listening."

Let us answer Your call as Isaiah did: "Here am I. Send me."

Let us willingly abandon our plans to follow after you, just as the disciples left all they knew for that opportunity.

Help us never be deterred by the uncertainty that awaits us in following You, but allow us to be driven by Our faith in the One who has called us.

You are the King of our home. Come, Lord.

Amen.

Praying for Marriages

This is why a man leaves his father and mother and bonds with his wife, and they become one flesh.
(Genesis 2:24)

Gracious Father, I thank You today for the structure of family as You designed it to be. I thank You for the gift of marriage, and the illustration it provides of Your love for Your Church. Thank You for the level of intimacy – spiritual, emotional, and physical – that is possible in the relationship of marriage. Thank You for designing us for such closeness with another person. Thank You for showing us the importance of marriage by making the very first human relationship one of marriage between a man and a woman.

I thank You for my marriage today, Lord. Thank You for bringing my husband and me together in a bond that cannot be broken. As we move through this life as one, help us daily to lay aside our personal, selfish desires in favor of seeking the best for each other. Let us both be willing to sacrifice ourselves, understanding that marriage isn't designed to make us happy but to make us holy. Please let our marriage be a vessel of sanctification, day by day making us more like Christ as we walk in Your ways. Let our marriage reflect Your love for us as shown in Jesus, and let us bear fruit for You through our union.

Show us what it really means to love another person, looking to your example for how to love in actions and truth, rather than with words and speech.

Father, You have given Your beloved child to me in marriage, and I pray that I would love him to the best of my ability. Mold me into the wife that he needs. I pray that I would honor and respect and submit to him as the Church submits to the leadership of Jesus. Help me to fill the role of helper to him that I was designed to be, respecting him in my words and actions. You have said that it is not good for man to be alone, so let me be what my husband needs me to be. I pray against selfishness, idolatry, immorality, temptation, dishonesty, and any other fruit of the flesh that could distort the image of Christ and the Church as represented in our marriage. Please forgive me for taking marriage lightly at times, and for not always seeking to represent You in our relationship.

Lord God, I pray for my husband, that he would learn by Your power to love me as You do. I pray for his leadership in our marriage, that You would be at the center of every decision he makes for our family. Help him to be a man of integrity, loving and cherishing me with the same unconditional love that Christ has for His Church.

And Father, please protect our marriage. Marriage as You created it to be is under attack by our enemy. He seeks to unravel the Church by creating disunity in the home. Protect us, Lord, as he seeks to tear us apart. Help us to lean on You, and never let us become complacently convinced that our relationship is invincible.

Father God, I also pray for the future marriages of my children. I pray for their spouses even now, wherever they are and whatever their lives look like now. I pray for Godly influences on them, that as they grow and their paths begin to converge, they would be prepared for the holy commitment of marriage. I pray that my marriage with my husband would be the kind of marriage that makes my children want to get married, and I pray that in everything we do together we would set a holy example for what marriage can and should be.

Lord God, You are so wise to create the covenant of marriage, knowing that we would not reach our full potential if we went through life alone. Thank You for giving us an intimate companion to walk with through our lives, and help us to always love as You first loved us.

You are the King of our home. Come, Lord.

Amen.

Praying for a Godly Community

Two are better than one.
(Ecclesiastes 4:9)

Heavenly Father, I thank You for creating us the way that You did – not to do life alone, but to walk alongside other people in close relationships. Because two are better than one, thank You for the people You bring into our lives. May we never take them for granted.

God, I pray that You would bring a steady stream of godly influences into the lives of my husband and children. Let them seek out other people to do life with. Please guard them against any tendencies of isolation or solitude, but remind them that they are made for community. Surround them with like-minded people who also have their hearts and eyes set on You, and build relationships of accountability. Let my family be receptive to advice and correction that comes from Your truth.

Lord God, I pray that You would cultivate relationships with godly men in my husband's life. Surround him with coworkers, church members, friends, and family members who challenge him in his faith. No one is strong enough to withstand cultural influences on their own, so I pray that the influences around my husband would be those that lead him closer to You. I pray that he and the friends You give him would be honest and vulnerable with each other, allowing for accountability that makes them more like Christ. As iron sharpens iron, may He be spurred on in his character and relationship with You through his relationships with others.

Father, please help my children to be surrounded by godly community. Bring friends and mentors into their lives that help them to reach the full potential that You have placed inside them. Surround them with people who have their hearts and minds set on You. Help them to gravitate toward those friends who will help them to make wise decisions, rather than to those who live in the ways of the world.

Lord, You tell us that it is not good for us to be alone. Let us always seek out encouraging community and fellowship, learn what it means to bear another's burdens, and experience what it means to allow other people into our lives. Lead us into the Body of Christ, that we will be living out Your true design for our lives.

You are the King of our home. Come, Lord.

Amen.

Praying for Protection from Evil

Submit to God. Resist the devil, and he will flee from you.
(James 4:7)

Merciful Father, I thank You today that no matter how much this life may feel like a battle, we are assured that the victory is Yours. Thank You for being our warrior King who goes into battle for us. Thank You for being not only the God of angel armies, but the God of every temptation and struggle we face. In You we find refuge and strength. You are our stronghold in the midst of every battle.

Lord, I pray today that You would continually fight for my family I pray that my husband and children would submit every battle to Your leadership. Teach them not to fight for themselves, but to submit themselves your commands...Your rules...Your battle strategy, that their enemy would have no choice but to flee. You are greater than any battle and any enemy they face, and with Your Spirit inside them they have assured victory over he who is in the world. Let him flee from them, Lord.

Gracious God, I pray for my husband and the specific evil that seeks him out every day simply because he is a man. I pray against the plots and schemes of the enemy to make him fall. The enemy knows his weak places and aims flaming arrows at those things with the intention of destroying him. The enemy uses an arsenal of lies, so I pray against the thoughts that are so easy to believe. Help him to stand firm in You, putting on his armor and raising his weapon at Your command and fighting as a soldier of heaven. Let him not back down in matters of character or integrity, but let him always be a shining example of Christlike manhood. As he pursues your will for his life, help me to be the supportive helpmate for him that You have designed me to be, and never let evil drive a wedge between us in our marriage.

Lord, I pray for my children as they grow up in a world with visible, tangible evidence of evil that the world hasn't seen before. But there is nothing new under the sun, and the forms of evil that manifest themselves in our world today are just a continuation of the same evil that has pervaded the world since the Fall. Father, as heartbreaking as it is for me to see the condition of the world into which I have brought my children, I know it breaks Your heart even more. I pray that they would stand firm in what they know of You, and would submit their lives to your leading. Father, that submission is counter-cultural, but it is the only way for them to walk in confidence and to send the enemy fleeing. Protect my children, Lord, as only You can.

Lord, the enemy comes like a prowling lion to steal, kill, and destroy anything that is good or noble in our lives. As Jesus prayed, I pray not that You would remove my family from the world, but that You would protect them from the evil one. Any attack of the enemy that is intended for our harm, use instead for our benefit. Help us to know Your voice and discern it from the other voices vying for our attention, desiring to lead us into destruction.

Father, please protect my family from evil. Guard our home, from corner to corner, wall to wall, floor to ceiling. Shield our eyes. Guard our hearts. Lead us in our words and our actions, that nothing we do would allow the devil to gain a foothold and have a place in our lives that is rightfully Yours. We are Yours, God, and we submit to You alone.

You are the King of our home. Come, Lord.

Amen.

Praying for Health

I pray that you are prospering in every way and are in good health.
(3 John 1:2)

Gracious Father, I thank You for the way that You have made our bodies. Even when we don't feel well or are having health issues, our bodies are so perfectly intricate and show the masterful design of Your hand. You are a wonderful Creator; I am continually in awe of the way that You have knit us together from conception, and hold us together even now.

Lord, today I pray for the health of my family. When we are unwell, it is hard to think about much else, so I ask You today to strengthen the bodies of my husband and children. Shield them from disease and illness, and help them to do their part to maintain a healthy lifestyle. Help them do what they can to care for their bodies, glorifying You in how they eat and drink. Let them establish healthy habits in moderation, having self-control and seeking fulfillment in You alone. Help them to see their physical bodies as temples of their spiritual selves – and even more, as temples of Your Holy Spirit.

I pray for the proper functioning of all their bodily systems. I pray that from the smallest cells to the most complex organs, their bodies would do their jobs to keep them in good health. Keep them mentally and physically healthy, that one would not negatively affect the other.

I pray that when unwell days come, my husband and children would continue to lean on You for strength. No matter what may be diagnosed or treated, I pray against despair and frustration. I pray for hope and encouragement and peace. Let their journey through illnesses big and small be an indication to the watching world of where their hope is.

When they are in need of medical help, I pray that You would lead us to the doctors and medications that will best provide healing. Thank You for the wisdom You have given in the miracle of modern medicine.

But God, I do ask You to keep my family healthy. You know how hard it is for me when there is illness in our home. By Your grace, please grant my family good health, and let us be thankful for every day that we feel good. Thank You for the bodies You created. Help us to steward them well.

You are the King of our home. Come, Lord.

Amen.

Praying for Pure Thoughts and Good Attitudes

Finally, brothers and sisters, whatever is true, whatever is honorable, whatever is just, whatever is pure, whatever is lovely, whatever is commendable – if there is any moral excellence and if there is anything praiseworthy – dwell on these things.
(Philippians 4:8)

Heavenly Father, I thank You today for the way that You have made us, with the ability to think and reason unlike any other of Your creations. I thank You for the complexity of our minds and the ways that You have uniquely designed each person in accordance with Your purposes for them.

I pray today for the minds of my family, God. There is an obvious connection between the thoughts a person has and the fruit that person's life bears, so I pray for Your Spirit to pervade every thought my husband, my children, and I have. I pray, Lord, that our minds would be fixed on things above – not on earthly things – that we would not be distracted by the chaos of life and how things appear.

Lord God, please help my family's thoughts to be in line with Your thoughts. Help my husband and children to choose truth over lies...the noble over the immoral...the right things over the wrong things...the pure over the corrupted...the lovely over the tainted...the admirable over the disapproved...the excellent over the easy....and the praiseworthy over the tolerable. Father, our minds have choices with every waking moment. We can wander into dangerous territory in our minds before our feet have taken a single step. Let us begin each journey, big or small, by taking the correct first step in our minds. We give You control over our minds, God, taking every thought captive and submitting them to You. Only You can keep our thoughts where they need to be.

God, I pray for the attitudes of my family. I pray, Lord, that whatever may come during their days, they would fix their eyes on You. I pray that Your Spirit would shine in them even when they are frustrated, disappointed, aggravated, angry, or discouraged. I pray that their attitude would be like that of Christ Jesus, willingly facing whatever comes their way simply out of submission to You.

I pray for the attitude of my husband and my children, that in all situations they would assume the best and see the good. I pray that they would enter every day with optimism, recognizing the potential in every situation in the same way You do, and look back on the day with gratitude for how You have worked. In all things, help their thoughts and attitudes be rooted in love, rather than fear or doubt or self-interest.

Father, You fight for my family. Guard their hearts. Guard their minds. Let them not be conformed to the ways this world thinks and acts, but let them be transformed as their minds are renewed by Your Spirit.

Lord, I want my family's lives to produce good fruit, and I know that depends on the health of their thoughts. Let my family's thoughts and attitudes be in keeping with that of Jesus, not that their lives would be perfect but that they would bring honor to You in every circumstance.

You are the King of our home. Come, Lord.

Amen.

Praying for Generosity and Stewardship

Do not store up for yourselves treasures on earth, where moth and rust destroy and where thieves break in and steal. But store up for yourselves treasures in heaven, where neither moth nor rust destroys, and where thieves don't break in and steal. For where your treasure is, there your heart will be also.
(Matthew 6:19-21)

Merciful Father, I thank You today for Your incredible generosity to us. Lord, You lavish blessings on me and have given me more than I could ever ask for. It is Your heart to give to the ones You love, and I thank You for the ways You pour out amazing things on us. Please forgive me for the ways I so often overlook the things You give, simply because in my limited sight it doesn't seem like enough or what I expected. Help me to see every gift You give as the perfect love gift of the perfect kind at the perfect time.

Father, I pray that You would cultivate in my family a spirit of generosity that reflects both Your heart and hearts of genuine gratitude. Help my husband, my children, and I to be characterized more by what we want to give away than what we want to accumulate. Let us live with open hands, cheerfully and lovingly giving of what we have to those who are less fortunate. But, God, please don't allow us to give in ways that are showy or for recognition. Let us give in secret, knowing that You see and that is enough.

God, help my family to not to be materially focused. It is easy for us to look around and see things that we think we need, but God, I pray against that tendency. The appetite for more is a hard one to tame and an impossible one to satisfy, but I pray that by Your Spirit at work within our home my family would rise above that craving. Lord, You have told us not to store up for ourselves treasures here on earth, because those things are not what matter and will not last. Embed that truth into our the mentality of my family so that no matter what we see around us...no matter what commercials say...no matter what other people have or are doing with their money, we would be unimpressed and unmoved.

Please, Father, help us not to be distracted by the glitz and glamor of our consumer-driven world. Help us to keep our eyes on You above all else.

Lord, I pray that my husband and children would increase in their spirits of generosity. Help my husband to pursue ways to bless others with what You have given us, rather than to pursue ways to bless ourselves. Please give him opportunities to be an example of generosity in a greedy world, without shining a light on him as the generous one. Help him to give all glory to You.

Father God, I pray that my children would grow up seeing generosity modeled in our home and would learn habits of giving. Please shield them from the materialism of the world, preventing them from being obsessed with possessions. Help them to learn what really matters, and to live life searching for ways to pour into the lives of others.

Please cultivate a real sense of contentment in our home, Lord. Help us all to look around us and appreciate all that we have without seeing what is missing. Help us to keep only the things we use and need, holding our possessions with a loose grip and releasing them when the time or the need arises. Lord, all that we have is from You and belongs to You. Help us to really believe that and to live like we know it is true.

You are the King of our home. Come, Lord.

Amen.

Praying for Gratitude and Thankfulness

Give thanks to the Lord, for He is good. His faithful love endures forever.
(Psalm 136:1)

Gracious Father, You have given so much from Your character of extravagant generosity. You have poured out blessing upon blessing, not because I have earned or deserve it, but because You love me and delight in doing so. You are a giving Father, and You are good.

In every moment, You are good.

In every situation, You are good.

In every thought You have about me, You are good.

In every purpose You have for my life, You are good.
When things around me don't look the way I think they should, Lord, You are good.

When I don't understand, You are good. When I don't know what to think or which way to go or why things are going the way they are, one thing I do know is that You are good.

In all things, at all times, Lord, You are good. Your name alone inspires praise.

Thank You, Lord, for the blessings You have given me in my family. It is humbling to take a step back and look at my life from a distance, recognizing all that You have brought into my life out of the goodness of Your heart.

My husband is a gift from You. You have placed him in my life for a reason, and even though marriage is hard and demands things from me that I feel inadequate to give, I know that You have designed it for my benefit. Thank You for my husband, God. Thank You for my marriage. Please let me never take him for granted, and never let me become complacent or lazy about our relationship. Please help me to always recognize it as the sacred union You intend it to be. Thank You, Lord, for my husband.

My children are a gift from You. You have chosen me to be their mother on purpose, even though I so often feel like I don't have what it takes to raise them right. You have given them to me and me to them, and You don't make mistakes. Help me to always remember that You gave me a treasured gift when You gave me the honor of being called "mom." Never let me begrudge this position. Thank You for trusting me with Your children, and please give me the strength to do what is being asked of me. Thank You, Lord, for my children.

Father, Your love for me endures forever. I love You, Lord, and as You have abundantly blessed me, I pray that my life would be poured out as a blessing to You. You are good, Lord, and it is my joy to serve You in my family. Be glorified in my life.

You are the King of our home. Come, Lord.

Amen.

Praying for Daily Needs

Anger and Unforgiveness

Lord God, You are a God of peace and unity, but a spirit of anger and bitterness has taken up residence in our home. Let Your peace come, easing tempers and helping us to be slow to speak in our frustration. Help us to assume the best about one another, rather than believing the worst and immediately becoming defensive and angry. When we become angry, help us not to sin but to resolve the conflict quickly and in love. Give us the humility of heart we need to admit when we are wrong, and to seek forgiveness when it is due. Let us offer forgiveness generously, remembering the forgiveness we have received in Christ. Give us the desire to keep unity and peace as the theme of our family, that our home will not be divided by bitterness. Banish the spirit of anger, Lord. Be near, Lord Jesus. Amen.

Anxiety and Fear

Father God, You are love, and perfect love knows no fear. Let my husband and children live without fear of the future or things unknown, knowing that nothing is hidden from Your sight and nothing surprises You. Help them to remember that whatever comes, You will be with them. Help them to find refuge in You, Lord, resting in Your constant presence and allowing You to fight for them. Help my family to never fear, but instead trust in Your constant presence and care. Let there be no place for fear or anxiety in our home. Be near, Lord Jesus. Amen.

Authority

Majestic God, You are over all and in all and it is all for You. You are our ultimate authority, and in Your wisdom You have placed certain people in authority as well. As You have given them the responsibility of governing and leading and making decisions that affect us all, You have given us the command to pray for them. We confess that this is hard, as we don't always agree with what they are doing. It is Your command, though, so we do pray for wisdom, humility, and strength for our leaders. Whether the authority they have been given is over a classroom of children or a nation of millions, we thank You for them and for their willingness to step into leadership. Be near to them, Lord, and be near to us as we respect the authority they have been given. Amen.

Bullying

Lord Jesus, You came to earth to show us what love looks like. Sadly, our selfish and sinful spirits too often seek our own way rather than the way of perfect love. As my children face the reality of bullying every day, help them to stand firm in their identity as Your child. Let them fight back only with the strength of love, not hating but having compassion on those who hurt them. Protect them from harm, Lord. Guard their bodies from injury, but guard their hearts and minds from lies and darkness. Work in the hearts of those who are causing this pain. Be near and do what You do as the Prince of Peace. Amen.

Competitiveness

Lord, the spirit of competitiveness is becoming obvious in my home. It is easy to put oneself above others, never assuming the lower position, but help my husband and children to do nothing out of their own selfish ambition and desire to be "the best". Help them to see others as better than themselves. Let them test their own hearts and see their own work through Your eyes, that they will boast only in what they have done and not in how that compares to others. Help them to take the subservient attitude of Christ. Be near, Lord, and change their hearts. Amen.

Critical/Judgmental Spirit

Lord, please guard my family from a spirit of negativity and criticism. There is a tendency to see only the bad in different situations and people, and I pray against that. Before they take a prideful view of any circumstance, I pray that my family would humble themselves. Convict them of their own sin and weaknesses, that they would see others with a new perspective of compassion. Give them a more optimistic view, seeing the potential in everything and everyone. Help them always to believe the best and watch for Your hand at work. Be near, Lord. Amen.

Depression

Lord, the grip of depression is real. Be near to the brokenhearted within my home, Jesus, and hear their cries. Hear them even when they don't know how to pray or have the strength to cry. Answer them quickly. Let them experience Your faithful love every morning. Grow their trust in You, leading them into the perfect peace that surpasses all understanding. Breathe life into the numbness, God, and hope into the darkness. Be near, Lord Jesus. Amen.

Disobedience

Father, my family is struggling with my child's disobedience – the deliberate decision to rebel against what is right. I know, God, that this is nothing new, and that disobedience has characterized the human race since the very beginning, but it takes on a whole new meaning when I see it day in and day out with my own child. God, I ask You to please do a new thing in my child's heart. Create in him a new heart, and renew his desire to do what is right. Draw him ever closer to Your heart. Give me the wisdom I need to raise him up in the way he should go, and help my family to remain in Your Spirit as we walk through this difficult season. Amen.

Fighting

Lord God, it is never Your desire that Your children would allow division and strife to set in. An angry tone has been set in my home, though, leading to all forms of anger, dissension, hatred, and strife. The works of the flesh have taken over. Help my family to avoid foolish debates and quarrels, realizing their fruitlessness, but instead to seek the way of peace and love. Unite our family in a new way, God, and make fighting a thing of the past. Be near. Amen.

Friends (Making Poor Choices)

Father, I see my children making poor choices about with whom they will spend their time. As iron sharpens iron, so, too, will bad company corrupt good morals. Help my children to see the foolishness of surrounding themselves with bad influences, and help them desire wholesome, edifying friendships that encourage them to become who You made them to be. Let them desire relationships that draw them closer to You. Be near in their schools and social situations, God. Help them to hear Your voice. Amen.

Gifted Child

Creator God, You have knitted my child together just as You intended. You are acquainted with the most intricate parts of who she is, and You know the way her brain works. Lord, parenting a gifted child presents struggles of its own. Please give me the wisdom to parent this child in a way that steers her toward Your perfect plans for her life. Her intelligence is a gift, and I pray it would always be nurtured. Help her, though, to not fall into perfectionism but to we comfortable with her weaknesses. Give her rest when her mind won't stop and when she puts pressure on herself to do more than might be possible. Be near, Lord, and help us both to navigate these tricky waters. Amen.

Idolatry

God, the word idolatry seems outdated, but the reality of it is not. There are thousands of things vying for my family's attention and affection, many of which offer immediate gratification. Help them to withstand the temptation to put those things at the center of their lives. Put to death their earthly natures that manifest in idolatry. Help them to recognize the idols in their lives and flee from them. Lead them find fulfillment in You alone. Refocus their affections and center their attention on You. Be near, Lord, and help them to crave Your presence above all else. Amen.

Illness

Merciful God, You have, in Your tremendous wisdom, created our bodies to work perfectly. At times, though, we are affected by the fact that we live in a sinful world. I pray today that You would heal the illness in my home. You tell us that Christ has overcome every struggle we will face in this world, so I pray for an overcoming over this sickness. I pray for healing and a strengthening of the physical body. As the body is weak, though, I pray that Your strength would be made perfect, showing us Your majesty and mercy in every situation. Be near, Lord, as my family faces this illness, and bring healing. Amen.

Lack of Discipline

Creator God, You have given us Your Spirit that we may be self-disciplined in every aspect of our lives. In Your name, we have a Spirit of power, love, and self-discipline. That means that we are not subject to the distracted, disorganized ways of the flesh, but that we can remain focused on forming good habits and ways of life. Lord, as You originally created man to live a self-disciplined life, restore that ability to my family. Help us to remain focused on You and on the power You have given us. Be near Lord, and may Your presence make us disciplined in how we approach this life You have given us. Amen.

Laziness

Lord, we were not originally created for hard work and the tediousness of so many aspects of life. However, the introduction of sin into the world made work both a requirement and a burden. Our flesh presses against the constant things to be done, and while rest is essential, laziness is a sin. Help my family to work at those things that are a struggle as though they are working for You; let that give them the motivation to work with excellence. As a slacker cannot find fulfillment for his cravings, God, I pray that my family would find no satisfaction in laziness. Be near, Lord, and help us feel Your powerful presence in all we do. Amen.

Loneliness

God, You see us when no one else does, and are our companion through our loneliest days. Help us to remember that, Lord, and to believe it in real ways. While no one else may stick around, You are here. You are with us. You care, and You weep when we weep. God, heal the loneliness my family feels. Bring human companionship and the kinds of relationships for which we were made. Be near, Lord, and in this time of loneliness, help us to feel You more than ever. Amen.

Marriage Trouble

Father, You have given me my spouse as a gift to make me a more complete reflection of who You are. Rather than seeing one another that way, though, we have allowed petty arguments and bitter anger to come between us. You have joined us together, but these things threaten to tear us apart. Help us to choose love in every situation, allowing the decision to love to overcome all offenses. Give us the strength to love one another as You have loved Your Church. Help us not to lose sight of why we got married. Be near, and help us in every interaction to listen and assume the best about one another. Amen.

Peer Pressure

Father, I ask You now to place a shield around my child, covering her with Your wings and creating a safe refuge for her. The power of peer pressure is closing in on her, and she needs Your strength to withstand it. I pray first, Lord, that she would have the desire to go against what her peers are saying and do, and then that she would have the strength of character to stand and do what is right. Help her to know she is fearfully and wonderfully made, and that only You can know what is best for her. Shield her, Lord, and help her to become the person You created her to be. Amen.

Perfectionism

Holy God, You are perfect in all Your ways. You created us to reflect You, but our pride got in the way and continues to destroy the joy You want for us. As perfectionism has taken up root in my home, I pray for humility and an acceptance of human weakness. I pray for an understanding that no human can be perfect, but that Your glory is shown in our weaknesses. In our desire for perfection, help us to listen to correction and be open to advice from others. Teach us what it means to have limits, and help us to be patient with ourselves. Be near, Lord, and let Your compassion overflow. Amen.

Repentance

Lord Jesus, You see the hearts of each one of us, and You see the sin that You came to erase. I pray now that my family would see their sin, too. They know what is right and what is wrong; sadly, they have chosen the latter. Convict them in the deepest parts of their hearts. Your Word promises, God, that when we come to You with humble, repentant hearts You are faithful to forgive. Please help my family come to You in confession and to receive Your forgiveness without shame or guilt. Lead their hearts to repentance, Lord, that they may move closer to You and to the people You have created them to be. Be near, Lord, and change their hearts. Amen.

Self-Care

Creator God, You have masterfully created our bodies for Your purposes, but we confess that we have not treated them as the masterpieces You say they are. We have chosen the lazy route, which, as it turns out, is sometimes the busy route. We have chosen to put other things above care for ourselves, and that has led to physical, mental, and spiritual exhaustion. We know, Lord, that this is not Your will for us. As our bodies are temples of Your Spirit, help us to treat them as such. Help us to be motivated to eat well...rest more intentionally...exercise more regularly...spend time with You more faithfully. Help us to care for ourselves as we would insist others care for themselves, that we might be better equipped to do the things You have planned for us. Be near, Lord, and speak to us in our busyness. Amen.

Self-Image

Precious Jesus, You chose to come to rescue us. Father God, You chose to adopt us as Your sons and daughters. It is so hard, though, to see ourselves as You see us. The words go in one ear and out the other as we look in the mirror or compare ourselves to what we see in other people. I pray, Lord, for the self-image of my family members. Help them to look at themselves with fresh eyes, recognizing and believing what You say about them. Guard their hearts against lies and half-truths that speak to their identities, and help them to find their self-image and their self-worth in You. Be near, Lord, and whisper Your truths. Amen.

Separation Issues

Lord God, You are a Father, so You know how it hurts when a child fights for their independence. For me, though, as a mama, it hurts when my children won't accept the independence that's appropriate for their ages. They are anxious, God, clinging to me for security, and while part of me loves that I am their safe place, part of me longs for them to be brave enough to do the hard thing. Help my children to sense Your presence, and let that be more than enough. As I remind them that they don't go into any situation alone, help them to absorb that truth and be empowered by it. Let them be strong, courageous, and firm as they separate, and help them not to fear. Be near them, Lord, as You have promised. Amen.

Special Needs Child

Father God, my child needs Your touch. I need Your touch. I need wisdom and guidance and patience to be the mama I need to be for my child. Her needs are so great, and my ability to meet them is so limited. Help me to serve my child and advocate for them, believing every moment that You have a plan for their lives, and that this weakness and struggle will be used for Your glory. Help me not to grow weary or impatient, but give me the strength to remember what You say: that my service to those who are suffering is service to You. Thank You for believing in me and for deliberately choosing me to parent this child. Be near, and make me who she needs me to be. Amen.

Spiritual Warfare

Holy Spirit, the war with our spiritual enemy is real and it is raging in our home. Come, Holy Spirit, and enable us to fight the real enemy and to fight with the weapons You have given us. Help us in every moment to be sober-minded and alert, as the enemy prowls around us looking for someone to devour. He has come to steal, to kill, and to destroy, but the One who is in us – YOU – are greater than he is. Give us strength for the battle and resilience against attack. Let us stand firm in the belief that You fight for us and with us, and that while the battle rages, the war is already won. Be near us in battle, Lord, and bring Your victory. Amen.

Straying from God

Gracious Father, one of Your children is wandering from You, and it breaks my heart. Please, God, bring them back to a fear of You and a desire for Your presence. As the prodigal son eventually returned home, help this prodigal to return to You. Keep him safe as he wanders, and bring him home humbly and without harm. Thank You for Your promise of accepting those who wander off; I pray now that You would go in search of the one You have lost. Be near, Lord, and draw Your prodigal back to You. Amen.

Stress

Lord, the burden of life is so heavy at times, and the pressure and stress can be overwhelming. Please be present in our home as my family faces the stress of everyday life. You have promised to be with us as the waters rage around us, and You have promised that we will not be overwhelmed. Help us, then, to accept the peace You offer and not be troubled by what we face. Help us to see the bigger picture, believing that these trials are strengthening us. Hold us up in the stress, Lord. Be near, and take this burden from us. Amen.

Strong-Willed Child

Father God, You surely know what it is like to parent a strong-willed child. We have pushed and rebelled and run from everything You have told us, yet in Your faithfulness You persist in loving us and pursuing us. Help me, God, to be the mama that my strong-willed child needs me to be. Please give me the wisdom to channel this strong, independent gift in the right ways. You have a masterful plan for his life, and I pray that nothing would squelch the strong will and singlemindedness You have given him. Let him instead be receptive to correction. As I do my best to raise my child in the way I want him to go, guide him by Your Spirit to not depart from it. Be near, Lord, giving me wisdom and giving my child direction. Amen.

Surrender

Lord, I lift up my family today in humility of spirit. I recognize that I can only do so much for them, and that it is You and only You who can change their hearts and cultivate lasting fruit in them. As I give them to You and submit them to Your will for their lives, I pray that You would do what I cannot for them. Amen.

Tension in the Home

Lord, You are a God of peace. You give peace unlike anything the world gives, and it is Your desire that we would live in peace and unity with one another. However, human nature creates tension. We find things to fuss and fight about, allowing bitterness to set in and affect the entire mood of our home. Please forgive us, and please help us to live differently than the rest of the world. Help us to believe the best, looking humbly and compassionately on one another. Help us to be quick to listen and slow to speak. Let us not jump straight to anger, but humbly consider the other person before ourselves. Be near, Lord, and ease the tension that has come over our home. Amen.

Trouble in School

God of all creation, You have made my children for a purpose. You have a perfect plan for their lives, yet they are struggling under the expectations of what is required for them at school. Help them, Lord, to have a sound mind and self-control, that nothing can distract them from what they are there to do. Please show their teachers how to work with them in the best way for them, and help me to be an encourager. Show me how to challenge my children without pressuring them to be different. Do a new thing in my children, Lord, and lead them in the paths of understanding. Amen.

Ungratefulness and Complaining

Father God, You have given us so much. You have provided in ways we cannot fathom, yet we – in our selfishness – have found reason upon reason to complain. Please forgive us for our ingratitude. You ask us to give thanks in everything, never grumbling or complaining regardless of the situation. Help my family to live up to that standard, and help my family to stand out in our generation as a family who is truly content. Give us hearts of true gratitude. Be near, Lord, and convict our greedy hearts. Amen.

Praying the Names and Attributes of God

El Shaddai

"Lord God Almighty", placing emphasis on His omnipotence (Genesis 17:1)

> El Shaddai, You are the most high. You are the almighty God, and Your hand holds my family. Because of Who You are as our omnipotent Father, I bow to You and surrender my family to Your power. Amen.

El Elyon

"The Most High God", indicating that He is the ultimate authority. There is none higher. (Genesis 14:17-20)

> El Elyon, You are the ultimate authority in my life. Forgive me, Lord, for the countless times I have taken the reins and tried to be my own god. There is none higher in my life, and I submit to You. Amen.

Adonai

"Lord and Master", acknowledging His authority over our lives. (Genesis 15:2)

Adonai, You are my Lord and my Master. I desire Your will before my own or any other. You have authority in my life, and I pray for the strength to resist the temptation to place anything above You. Amen.

Yahweh

"God, Lord of all". Shows His authority over all creation and, by implication, our lives. (Genesis 2:4)

Yahweh, Lord of all, You have dominion over all creation. As Your created, beloved child, I am under Your authority and willingly submit to You. Amen.

Jehovah Nissi

"The Lord my Banner", referencing a flag or banner flown over warriors going into battle. Demonstrates that God fights for us. (Exodus 17:15)

Jehovah Nissi, you are my banner in the battle. As hard as I may fight, the battle is Yours. You fight for me, not only when I am at my limit, but as soon as the battle begins. I raise You high over my life. Amen.

Jehovah Raah

"The Lord my Shepherd", calling our attention to the care, protection, and discipline of God. (Psalm 23)

Jehovah Raah, You are my Shepherd, and I shall not want for anything. You care for me...protect me...discipline me in Your love. You are for me, and I will not forget that. I trust You to be gentle in Your care for me. Amen.

Jehovah Rapha

"The Lord that Heals", showing His unique ability to restore what is broken. (Exodus 15:26)

> Jehovah Rapha, You are the healing Father. You see the broken places in me and in my life and in my family, and I believe that You have the power, unlike any other, to restore them to wholeness. I give those broken places to You, trusting You to repair what I have broken. Amen.

Jehovah Shammah

"The Lord is Here", acknowledging His unwavering presence in times of trouble. (Ezekiel 48:35)

> Jehovah Shammah, You have never left me and You never will. Even when I feel alone and in despair, Your presence never wavers. You are with me. Always, You are with me. Help me to trust Your presence. Amen.

Elohim

"The One True God", indicating His unrivaled authority over the earth. (Genesis 1:1)

> Elohim, You and You alone are God over Your creation. There is no other god but You, and none can rival You in Your authority. Please forgive me for placing anything above Your in my heart. Amen.

Jehovah Jireh

"The Lord will provide", which shows trust in God's faithfulness. (Genesis 22:14)

> Jehovah Jireh, all that I have comes from You. You are faithful in everything, providing for my every need. You

know my heart, Lord, and I trust You to give only what is best. Amen.

Jehovah Shalom

"The Lord is peace", calling on His ability to speak peace into even the most troubled times. (Judges 6:24)

> Jehovah Shalom, You alone are my peace. You are my refuge in all storms and every battle. You are my stronghold and I rest in You. Amen.

Jehovah Sabaoth

"The Lord of Hosts" or "The Lord of Armies", who goes into battle before us. (1 Samuel 1:3)

> Jehovah Sabaoth, You are my shield in battle. You go before me into the war and make a way for me. You are my strength in my weakness, and I follow Your lead. Amen.

El Roi

"The God who sees me", showing faith that God loves us, understands us, and has not abandoned us. (Genesis 16:13)

> El Roi, You see me when no one else does. I cannot hide from You and I cannot outrun You. If I go to the depths of the sea, You will find me there. You understand me, Lord, and I am grateful. Amen.

I AM

A name God uses for Himself, revealing his eternal authority. (Exodus 3:14)

You are the Great I AM, Lord, and in saying so I recognize Your unique ability to give a name to Yourself. You are who You say You are. I believe You and I trust You. Amen.

Alpha and Omega

"Beginning and End", *acknowledging God's eternal nature. (Revelation 21:6)*

Alpha...Omega...You are my beginning and my end. You were present at my conception and will be there when I draw my last breath. You are everlasting, never-ending, unwavering in Your love for me. Thank You for the security that comes in knowing that while everything else will fall away, You never will. Amen.

Jehovah N'Kaddesh

"God who makes us holy", *calling upon God's unique ability to sanctify us and recreate us in the image of Jesus. (Exodus 31:13)*

Jehovah N'Kaddesh, You see me not only for who I am but for who I could be. You love me too much to leave me where I am and draw me continually into Your heart in order to change me. Recreate me now in the image of Your Son and lead me into Your will for my life.

El Olam

The Everlasting God, referencing the eternal faithfulness and authority of God. (Genesis 21:33)

El Olam, Your faithfulness will never change. You have proven Yourself, though You had no obligation to do so, and I submit to Your trustworthy authority. Amen.

El Gibhor

"The Warrior God", *claiming the willingness and power of God to go to battle for us.*

> El Gibhor, You go before me into every battle, not because You have to but because Your love for me compels You to do so. You are my strength, my shield, and my security. Amen.

Index of Scriptural References

Anger

James 1:19-20, Ephesians 4:26-31, Number 14:18, Psalm 4:4, Psalm 86:15, Ecclesiastes 7:9, Joel 2:13, Jonah 4:2, Nahum 1:3, 1 Timothy 2:8

Anxiety and Fear

Deuteronomy 31:6, Psalm 23:4, Joshua 1:9, Psalm 139:23, Proverbs 12:25, Philippians 4:6, Matthew 6:25-34, Luke 21:14-15, Job 39:22, Psalm 40:1-3, Psalm 91:1-6, Psalm 112:7-8, Isaiah 35:4, Isaiah 41:13, Haggai 2:5, Luke 1:73-75, 1 John 4:18, 1 Peter 5:7

Authority

1 Timothy 2:1-2, James 1:5-7, 2 Corinthians 2:9, Philippians 2:8, 1 Peter 1:14, Colossians 3:20, Colossians 3:22, Hebrews 13:17, 1 John 2:3, 1 John 5:3

Bullying

2 Timothy 1:7, 1 John 2:9, Galatians 5:22-23, Romans 11:22, 2 Samuel 10:2, Titus 3:4-5, Colossians 3:12, Ephesians 2:6-7

Competitiveness

Philippians 2:3-4, Galatians 6:4 (ESV), 1 Corinthians 1:31, Jeremiah 17:9, Philippians 4:8-9, Matthew 5:3, 1 Corinthians 13:1-13, 1 Corinthians 3:6-7, John 15:1-27, John 15:5

Critical Spirit

Matthew 7:1-5, James 4:6, Jeremiah 17:9, Romans 2:1-3, Ephesians 4:32, James 4:11, Matthew 7:1,

Depression

Psalm 34:17-18, Psalm 143:7-8, Isaiah 26:3, Isaiah 41:10-13, Matthew 11:28, Jeremiah 29:11, Psalm 30:5, Philippians 4:6-7, Psalm 9:9, Psalm 34:18, Revelation 21:4, Deuteronomy 31:6-8, Psalm 3:3, Psalm 30:11, Philippians 4:8

Faithfulness

See Fruit of the Spirit

Fighting

Galatians 5:19-24, Titus 3:10, Romans 12:16, 1 Peter 3:8, James 1:19-20

Friends

Proverbs 13:20, 1 Corinthians 15:33, 1 Timothy 4:12, Matthew 28:20, Psalm 27:10, Ecclesiastes 4:9-12, John 15:13, Proverbs 17:17, 1 Thessalonians 5:11, Proverbs 27:6, Hebrews 10:24-25, Romans 1:12, Luke 6:31, 1 Corinthians 13:1-13

Gentleness
See *Fruit of the Spirit*

Generosity/Stewardship
2 Corinthians 9:6-8, 1 John 3:17, Hebrews 13:16, Luke 12:33, Proverbs 19:17, Proverbs 21:13, Proverbs 22:9, Proverbs 28:27, 1 Timothy 6:17-19, Luke 21:1-4, Proverbs 11:24-25, Deuteronomy 15:7-8, Psalm 37:26, Psalm 112:5, Psalm 119:36, 2 Corinthians 9:11, Acts 20:35, Malachi 3:10, James 1:17, 1 John 4:19, Colossians 3:2, Deuteronomy 10:14

Gifted Child
Proverbs 1:8-9, 2 Corinthians 2:9-10, Psalm 139, Proverbs 22:6, Ephesians 6:1-4, Colossians 3:21, Proverbs 29:15, Proverbs 10:1

Godly Community
Proverbs 13:20, Ecclesiastes 4:9-12, 1 Corinthians 1:10, 1 John 1:7, 1 Thessalonians 5:14, Galatians 6:2, Proverbs 17:17, Proverbs 27:17, Philippians 2:3-16, Hebrews 10:24-25, 1 Corinthians 12:25-27, Romans 12:3-13, Acts 2:44-47, Matthew 18:20, Romans 12:5, Romans 12:16, Romans 1:11-12, John 15:12-13, Genesis 2:18

Goodness
See *Fruit of the Spirit*

Gratitude and Thankfulness
Colossians 1:12, Colossians 2:7, Colossians 3:15, Colossians 4:2, Hebrews 12:28, Hebrews 13:15, Psalm 7:17, Psalm 9:1, Psalm 35:18, Psalm 52:9, Psalm 69:30, James 1:17, Philippians 4:6,

Psalm 118:1, 29, Psalm 147:7, Revelation 11:17, Deuteronomy 10:14, Colossians 3:2, Matthew 7:11, John 10:10, Malachi 3:10, Psalm 136, Matthew 19:6, Philippians 4:13, Philippians 2:17

Health

1 Corinthians 6:19-20, Jeremiah 30:17, 1 Corinthians 10:31, 1 Timothy 4:8, Proverbs 17:22, Acts 27:34, Revelation 14:12, Proverbs 3:7-8, Romans 12:1-2, Proverbs 14:30, Psalm 63:5, Galatians 5:23, Psalm 139, Psalm 71:14

Hearts of Servants

Hebrews 6:10, Galatians 5:13, Romans 12:1, 1 Samuel 12:24, Romans 7:6, Hebrews 9:14, John 12:26, Joshua 22:5, Romans 12:11, 1 Chronicles, 28:9, Matthew 23:11, Mark 10:45, 1 Peter 4:10, Philippians 2:1-11, 1 Corinthians 12, 1 Corinthians 2:16, John 21:16, 1 John 3:1

Holy Spirit

Filling of: Luke 24:49, John 3:8, Romans 8:3-6, Micah 3:8, Acts 2:1-5, Genesis 1:2, Psalm 104:30, 1 Peter 3:8, Ezekiel 37:11-14, 1 Corinthians 2:4, Zechariah 4:6, Matthew 5:14-16, John 14:26, Exodus 13:21-22, 1 Corinthians 6:19, 2 Corinthians 5:7, Romans 6:12-23, Acts 2, Ephesians 4:30, Exodus 13:21, Joshua 1:9, John 8:32, 3 John 1:4,

Fruit of:

Love: Galatians 5:22, Ephesians 5:22-23, Ecclesiastes 4:9-12, Romans 12:9-10, Romans 13:8, Proverbs 17:17 Ephesians 4:2-3, 1 John 4:7-18, John 15:9-13, John 3:16, 1

John 3:1, 1 John 4:18, John 13:35, 1 Corinthians 13, John 15:4-6, John 15:13

Joy: Galatians 5:22, 1 Thessalonians 5:16-18, Zephaniah 3:17, Isaiah 61:10, Romans 12:12, Philippians 4:4, Psalm 118:24, Habakkuk 3:17-18, 1 Peter 1:8-9, Proverbs 15:23, Ecclesiastes 1:9, Colossians 3:2, Proverbs 15:13, Matthew 5:14-16, John 16:33, 2 Corinthians 4:16-18, Luke 22:41, 1 Thessalonians 5:5, 1 Thessalonians 5:16-18

Peace: Galatians 5:22, Colossians 3:15, 1 Peter 3:11, Mark 5:34, Luke 1:79, 1 Thessalonians 5:15, Philippians 4:7, Proverbs 12:20, Psalm 29:11, Romans 12:18, Isaiah 9:6, Isaiah 26:3, John 16:33, 1 Corinthians 14:33, Romans 8:31, Psalm 139:13, Philippians 1:6, Romans 8:31-39, 2 Corinthians 5:18-20, Matthew 11:28-30

Patience: Galatians 5:22-23, Ecclesiastes 7:9, Ephesians 4:2, Galatians 6:9, Genesis 29:20, 1 Corinthians 13:4, Philippians 4:6, Proverbs 15:18, Jeremiah 29:11, Romans 12:12, 1 Samuel 13:8-14, Romans 8:24-30, Psalm 75:2, Habakkuk 2:3, Romans 5:3-5, 2 Corinthians 12:9, 2 Corinthians 4:16-18

Kindness: Galatians 5:22-23, Romans 11:22, 2 Samuel 10:2, Titus 3:4-5, Colossians 3:12, Ephesians 2:6-7

Goodness: Galatians 5:22-23, Galatians 6:10, Romans 12:21, Romans 12:9, Nahum 1:7, 1 Corinthians 10:23, Psalm 25:6-7, Titus 2:14, Matthew 5:15-16, Psalm 37:3, 2

Peter 1:5-7, 2 Corinthians 9:8, Jeremiah 6:16, Psalm 34:14, 1 Corinthians 15:33, Psalm 27:13, 1 John 1:5, 1 Thessalonians 5:5, Ephesians 5:11, Romans 12:21

Faithfulness: Galatians 5:22-23, 3 John 3-4, 1 John 1:9, Luke 16:10, Hebrews 10:23, Ephesians 2:8, Proverbs 3:3, Proverbs 28:20, Lamentations 3:23, 1 Corinthians 1:9, 2 Thessalonians 3:3, 2 Timothy 2:13, Deuteronomy 7:9, Psalm 89:8, Matthew 7:24-27, Philippians 2:3-11, Matthew 6:33, Matthew 5:14-16, Matthew 25:21

Gentleness: Additional Scripture: Galatians 5:22-23, Colossians 3:12, Proverbs 15:1, Colossians 4:5-6, Leviticus 19:17-18, Galatians 6:10, Philippians 4:5, 2 Corinthians 10:1, James 3:17, Isaiah 40:11, 1 Kings 19:12, Matthew 11:29, Matthew 21:4-5, Romans 6:23, Matthew 5:5

Self-Control: Galatians 5:22-23, 2 Timothy 1:7, 1 Corinthians 10:13, Philippians 4:13, Proverbs 16:32, Titus 1:6-8, Romans 12:1-2, Philippians 4:8-9, 1 Peter 5:6-8, Ephesians 6:10-20, Titus 2, Luke 1:37, John 14:15-31, 2 Peter 1:3, Proverbs 4:23, James 3:1-12, 2 Corinthians 12:9, Philippians 4:13, Hebrews 12:2, John 16:33

Humility

2 Timothy 3:16, Proverbs 1:7, Colossians 3:12, Ephesians 4:2, Proverbs 11:2, Psalm 25:9, Romans 12:3, James 4:6, 1 Peter 5:5, Luke 14:11, Micah 6:8, Proverbs 3:34, Proverbs 12:15, Psalm 23, Genesis 1:1, James 4:10-14, Philippians 2:1-11, Proverbs 8:13, Proverbs 16:18, 1 Corinthians 1:31

Idolatry

Colossians 3:5, 1 Corinthians 10:14, Exodus 20:3-6, 1 John 5:21, Leviticus 19:4, Galatians 5:19-21, Psalm 135:15-18, Galatians 4:8, Judges 10:14, Romans 1:23, Micah 5:13, Isaiah 42:17, Acts 17:29

Illness

John 16:33, 2 Corinthians 12:9, Psalm 139, 1 Corinthians 6:19-20, Jeremiah 30:17, 1 Corinthians 10:31, 1 Timothy 4:8, Proverbs 17:22, Acts 27:34, Revelation 14:12, Proverbs 3:7-8, Romans 12:1-2, Proverbs 14:30, Psalm 63:5, Galatians 5:23

Joy
See *Fruit of the Spirit*

Kindness
See *Fruit of the Spirit*

Lack of Discipline

2 Timothy 1:7, Titus 1:8, 1 Corinthians 9:27, Proverbs 25:28, Hebrews 12:1-3, 1 Peter 4:7, Galatians 6:1, Proverbs 22:6, 2 Corinthians 10:5,

Laziness

Proverbs 13:4, Colossians 3:23, Proverbs 21:25-26, Proverbs 18:9, Isaiah 40:31, John 15:1-8

Living for God, Not Man

2 Peter 3:9, Romans 12:2, Matthew 22:37, Matthew 6:33, Matthew 6:24, Romans 14:8, Colossians 3:23, Psalm 73:26, Colossians 3:1-6, 1 Peter 2:15, John 15:18-19, 2 Corinthians 5:15, Exodus 20:3, Acts 17: 25-28, Ephesians 6:12, Philippians 1:21, Acts 5:29, Romans 8:7, Isaiah 14:27, John 10:10, Mark 8:36, 1 Corinthians 1:31, Philippians 2:13, Hebrews 4:15, Matthew 5:13-16

Loneliness

Matthew 28:20, Psalm 27:10, Proverbs 13:20, 1 Corinthians 15:33, 1 Timothy 4:12, Matthew 28:20, Psalm 27:10, Ecclesiastes 4:9-12, John 15:13, Proverbs 17:17, 1 Thessalonians 5:11, Proverbs 27:6, Hebrews 10:24-25, Romans 1:12, Luke 6:31, 1 Corinthians 13:1-13

Love

See *Fruit of the Spirit*

Marriages

Ephesians 5: 25-33, Ecclesiastes 4:9-12, Malachi 2:15, Song of Solomon 8:6, Ephesians 4:23, Mark 10:9, Galatians 5:19-25, 1 John 4:11-12, 1 John 2: 15-17, 1 John 4:19, Psalm 1:1-3, John 15:12, 1 Corinthians 13:1-13, 1 Corinthians 16:14, John 13:35, 1 John 3:18, Matthew 19:6, Genesis 2:18, Genesis 3:16,

Trouble In: Romans 12:16, Proverbs 10:12, Matthew 19:16, James 1:19-20, John 10:10

Patience
See *Fruit of the Spirit*

Peace
See *Fruit of the Spirit*

Perfectionism
Proverbs 1:8-9, 2 Corinthians 2:9-10, Philippians 3:12-14, 2 Samuel 22:31, Matthew 11:28, Philippians 2:3-4, Galatians 6:4 (ESV), 1 Corinthians 1:31, Jeremiah 17:9, Philippians 4:8-9, Matthew 5:3, 1 Corinthians 13:1-13, 1 Corinthians 3:6-7, John 15:1-27, John 15:5

Prayerfulness
Galatians 5:22-23, Romans 12:12, Psalm 5:3, Psalm 55:17, Luke 2:37, Psalm 109:4, Daniel 6:9-11, 1 Timothy 5:5, Psalm 105:4, John 15:5-8, Matthew 6:7, Mark 12:40, Luke 20:47, Mark 14:38, Luke 21:36, Colossians 4:2, Luke 18:1, James 5:17-18, 2 Kings 17:1, Psalm 18:1-3, Luke 5:16, Luke 11:2-4, Psalm 1:2-3

Protection from Evil
Isaiah 41:10, Psalm 91:1-4, 2 Thessalonians 3:3, Psalm 23:4, 2 Samuel 22:3-4, Psalm 46:1, Psalm 121, Proverbs 18:10, Genesis 50:20, 1 Peter 5:8, John 16:33, John 10:27-28, Deuteronomy 31:6, Psalm 57:1, 1 John 4:4, Ephesians 6:10-18, Proverbs 30:5, John 17:15, Exodus 14:14, Matthew 6:13, John 10:10, 1 Corinthians 15:57, Exodus 14:14, James 4:7, Deuteronomy 20:4, John 8:44, Psalm 44:5, Genesis 3:16, Proverbs 4:23, Matthew 5:14-16, James 4:7-10, Ephesians 4:27

Protection of Family Relationships

1 John 4:19, 1 Timothy 5:8, Acts 10:2, Ephesians 6:4, Exodus 20:12, Joshua 24:15, Proverbs 6:20, Psalm 127:3-5, 1 Corinthians 13:4-7, Colossians 3:20, Ephesians 6:1-2, Psalm 103:17, Proverbs 11:29, 1 Corinthians 1:10, Colossians 3:13-14, John 17:23, Psalm 133:1, Philippians 2:1-4, Ephesians 1:10, 1 Peter 3:8, 1 John 4:12, Ephesians 4:3, Romans 12:16, Genesis 2:24, James 1:17, 1 John 3:1, John 10:10, Romans 12:2, Mark 10:9, James 3:1-12, Ecclesiastes 4:12, Ephesians 6

Purpose and Calling

John 15:16, Romans 8:28, 1 Thessalonians 5:24, 1 Corinthians 1:28-29, Philippians 3:14, 1 Peter 2:21, 2 Timothy 1:9, Matthew 5:13-16, Exodus 9:16, Job 42:2, Proverbs 19:21, Philippians 2:12-13, 1 Samuel 3, Isaiah 6:8-9, Matthew 4:18-22, Isaiah 14:27, Ephesians 2:10, Philippians 2:13, 1 John 3:1, 2 Corinthians 5:11-21, Jeremiah 29:11, Psalm 90:12-17, Psalm 139:13, John 15:4

Repentance

1 John 1:9, James 4:17, Isaiah 53:6, Proverbs 1:7, 1 Timothy 2:4, Matthew 18:12-13, Luke 15:8-32

Resistance to Temptation

James 1:13-15, Luke 22:40, Matthew 6:13, Luke 11:4, Luke 4:13, Mark 8:11, Matthew 22:18, Proverbs 7:25-26, James 4:1-4, 1 Peter 4:12, 1 Timothy 6:9, Ephesians 6:10-18, Psalm 139:2, Genesis 3, 1 Corinthians 10:13, Luke 15:11-32, Romans 6:1-6, Hebrews 12:1-2, 1 Kings 19:12, John 10:27-28, 2 Corinthians 3:5, Hebrews 4:15m Matthew 4:1-11

Salvation
Isaiah 57:12, Matthew 19:25-26, Romans 3:23, Romans 8:38-39, Romans 10:9-10, Hebrews 7:25, John 19:28-30, Genesis 3, Psalm 16:11, Deuteronomy 32:21, Deuteronomy 28:1-2, Proverbs 22:6, Jeremiah 29:11, 2 Corinthians 5:16-20, John 3:16, Romans 6:23, John 10:10, 1 Kings 19:11-13, Romans 12:1-2, Psalm 119:11

Self-Control
See *Fruit of the Spirit*

Self-Care
1 Corinthians 6:19-20, Ephesians 2:10, James 4:17, Luke 5:16

Self-Image
John 1:12, Genesis 1:27, Psalm 139:13-14, 1 John 3:1, Ephesians 2:10, Jeremiah 1:5, Romans 5:8, Luke 12:6-7

Separation Issues
Deuteronomy 31:6, Joshua 1:9, Psalm 23:4, Psalm 139:23, Proverbs 12:25, Philippians 4:6, Matthew 6:25-34, Luke 21:14-15, Job 39:22, Psalm 40:1-3, Psalm 91:1-6, Psalm 112:7-8, Isaiah 35:4, Isaiah 41:13, Haggai 2:5, Luke 1:73-75, 1 John 4:18, 1 Peter 5:7

Special Needs Child
Jeremiah 29:11, Matthew 25:40, Psalm 139, James 1:27, Psalm 82:3, Matthew 6:1-4, Acts 20:35, Psalm 10:17

Spiritual Gifts

1 Corinthians 12:4-31, Romans 12:6-8, 1 Peter 4:10-11, Ephesians 4:11-16, 2 Timothy 1:6-7, 2 Corinthians 13, Joel 2:28, Ephesians 4:1, 2 Corinthians 14:1, Ephesians 2:10, 2 Corinthians 12:9, 1 John 4:18, 2 Corinthians 5:7, 1 Timothy 4:12, John 14:16, John 16:13, Acts 1:8, Philippians 2:13, Ephesians 2:10, Psalm 139:13

Spiritual Warfare

1 John 4:4, 1 Peter 5:8-9, Ephesians 6:10-20, 2 Corinthians 10:3-5, 1 John 5:4, James 4:7-8, Romans 8:31

Straying from God

Isaiah 53:6, Proverbs 1:7, 1 Timothy 2:4, Matthew 18:12-13, Luke 15:8-32

Strength in Difficult Times

Psalm 46:1-3, 1 Chronicles 16:11, Proverbs 18:10, Nehemiah 8:10, Isaiah 41:10, Exodus 15:2, Psalm 9:9-10, Deuteronomy 31:6, Deuteronomy 33:27, Hebrews 2:18, Hebrews 4:15, Philippians 4:6, John 14:27, Psalm 27:1-3, Isaiah 12:2, Psalm 138:3, Psalm 112:1, 2 Thessalonians 3:3, Philippians 4:13, 2 Corinthians 12:9, Isaiah 40:28-31, Hebrews 13:8, 2 Corinthians 12:8-10

Stress

James 1:2-4, John 14:27, Isaiah 43:1-2, Romans 8:31, Matthew 6:34, Luke 10:41-42, Hebrews 12:1-3

Strong-Willed Child

Proverbs 22:6, James 1:5-7, Proverbs 12:1, Jeremiah 29:11, Ephesians 6:4, Proverbs 29:15, Psalm 127:3, Ephesians 2:10

Surrender

James 1:22, James 4:7, James 4:10, Jeremiah 10:23, Matthew 11:28, Matthew 26:39, Proverbs 23:26, Psalm 46:10, Proverbs 3:5-6, 1 Peter 5:7, Psalm 4:5, Psalm 9:10, Psalm 13:5, Psalm 22:4, Psalm 25:1, Philippians 4:6-7, John 14:1, Psalm 31:14, Psalm 33:21, Psalm 56:3, Isaiah 40:31

Tension

Romans 12:16, 1 Peter 3:8, James 1:19-20, John 14:1, James 4:1, 1 Corinthians 13:1-13, Luke 17:3-4, , Romans 12:17-18, James 1:19, Proverbs 16:18, Ephesians 4:31

Thoughts/Attitude

Romans 12:2, 1 Timothy 1:7, Proverbs 28:26, Proverbs 4:23, Ephesians 4:22-32, Matthew 15:11, Psalm 42, Psalm 56:3-4, Psalm 100, 2 Corinthians 10:5 Proverbs 3:5, Colossians 3:2-5, Psalm 45:7, Romans 5:1-2, 1 John 4:8, Philippians 2:3-11, John 15:5, 1 Samuel 16:7, Matthew 5:14-16, 1 John 4:18, Romans 12:2

Trust in God

Psalm 33:4, 1 Peter 2:3, 1 Chronicles 16:11, Isaiah 41:10, Jeremiah 17:5, Isaiah 40:30-31, Romans 8:31-39, Romans 8:28, Jeremiah 29:11, 1 Timothy 2:3-4, Psalm 119:105, 2 Peter 3:9, Psalm 9:10, Psalm 16:5-11, Psalm 62:8, Psalm 27:1, Psalm 28:7, John 10:10, Psalm 18:30, 1 John 4:18, James 1:17

Ungratefulness

Philippians 2:14, 1 Thessalonians 5:16-18, Psalm 118:24, Matthew 6:21, Acts 24:3, Philippians 4:6-7, Philippians 4:12-13, Psalm 136, Psalm 103:2

Wisdom

James 1:5, Job 12:12, Psalm 37:30, Proverbs 1:7, Proverbs 3:7, Proverbs 4:6-7, Proverbs 13:1, 1 Corinthians 1:25, Colossians 2:2-3, James 3:17, Proverbs 19:20, Proverbs 3:13, Matthew 7:7, Isaiah 30:21, Psalm 1:3, Isaiah 55:8-9, Psalm 18:30, Isaiah 40:28, John 10:10, Job 28:28, Hebrews 12:2

In Decision-Making

Philippians 4:6-7, Proverbs 3:5-6, Proverbs 15:22, Proverbs 12:15, James 1:5, Psalm 37:4, 2 Peter 1:3, Colossians 3:17, Philippians 2:13, Proverbs 11:14, Psalm 119:105, Philippians 1:27

Notes for Personal Reference

Additional Resources for You

Batterson, Mark. *Praying Circles Around Your Children*. Zondervan, 2012.

Copeland, Germaine. *Prayers That Avail Much for Mothers.* 9th ed., Word Ministries, 1990.

Countryman, Jack. *Names of God: Exploring God's Character*. Thomas Nelson, 2008.

O'Martian, Stormie. *The Power of a Praying Mom: Powerful Prayers for You and Your Children*. Harvest House, 2015.

O'Martian, Stormie. *The Power of a Praying Parent.* Harvest House, 1995.

O'Martian, Stormie. *The Power of a Praying Wife.* Harvest House, 1997.

Shirer, Patricia. *Fervent: A Woman's Battle Plan for Serious, Specific, and Strategic Prayer*. B&H Publishing, 2015.

St. John, Heidi. *Prayers for the Battlefield: Staying Momstrong in the Fight for Your Family and Your Faith.*
Tyndale Momentum, 2018.

Wilkerson, David. *The Jesus Person Promise Book.* Baker, 1972.

Acknowledgements

Everyone always says in sections like this one (and in awards show acceptance speeches) that there are countless people to thank. As it turns out, there's a reason they say that: any endeavor of this magnitude involves a village of supporters.

Thank you...

...to Scott and Leah. You two are amazing. Thank you for believing in me...for giving me time and space to write...for being so gracious with my grumpy writer moods. You make me want to get this prayer thing down, once and for all. You're my favorites.

...to Mom and Dad, for always cheering me on. I've come up with some pretty random aspirations over the years, but you've never done anything but believe in me. Thank you.

...to Angelia and Ashley. I wouldn't be who I am without you. I'm so thankful God gave me you.

...to Mom B and Dad B. Thank you for encouraging me. I know I'm a little different, but I also know you're always in my corner. Thank you for always being available.

...to Grandaddy and Grandpa. I couldn't have done this without you, in the most literal sense. I wish you were here to see it.

...to Granny and Grandmother. You have always, always, always encouraged me to write. You were right: this is what I'm meant to do, for better or worse.

...to Faith, for being one of my biggest supporters and cheerleaders as I made my way through this process. I'm so thankful for your friendship, and I'm so proud of us. Together we can do the big things.

...to Lisa, who gets me like no one else does. I'm so thankful for you and the way you help me to see myself more clearly. Thank you for believing in me even when I can't.

...to my precious tribe. There are more of you than I could possibly mention. Thank you for letting me be me, and for loving me while I'm figuring out what that means.

...to Forrest. You taught me what prayer looks like in the real world, and because of you, I believe in the power of these words. Thank you.

And finally...
...to the kids of North Columbia Elementary. Thank you for relentlessly asking, "How's your book going?" Without your belief in me, I might have quit a long time ago. Don't give up on your dreams, guys. Anything is possible.

Jessica Bolyard is a Christ-following truth-teller who writes and speaks with transparency about mental illness and community. Her passion is helping other women discover the common threads that connect us all, and her favorite phrase is, "You're not the only one."

Connect with Jessica online at
JessicaBolyard.com
Instagram.com/Jessica_Bolyard
Facebook.com/JessicaBolyardWriter
disEntangled Podcast

58193595R00105

Made in the USA
Columbia, SC
17 May 2019